NEW DIRECTIONS FOR STUDENT SERVICES

Margaret J. Barr, *Northwestern University*
EDITOR-IN-CHIEF

M. Lee Upcraft, *The Pennsylvania State University*
ASSOCIATE EDITOR

New Roles for Educational Fundraising and Institutional Advancement

Melvin C. Terrell
Northeastern Illinois University

James A. Gold
State University of New York College at Buffalo

EDITORS

Number 63, Fall 1993

JOSSEY-BASS PUBLISHERS
San Francisco

NEW ROLES FOR EDUCATIONAL FUNDRAISING AND
INSTITUTIONAL ADVANCEMENT
Melvin C. Terrell, James A. Gold (eds.)
New Directions for Student Services, no. 63
Margaret J. Barr, Editor-in-Chief
M. Lee Upcraft, Associate Editor

Microfilm copies of issues and articles are available in 16mm and 35mm,
as well as microfiche in 105mm, through University Microfilms Inc., 300
North Zeeb Road, Ann Arbor, Michigan 48106.

LC 85-644751   ISSN 0164-7970   ISBN 1-55542-680-8

NEW DIRECTIONS FOR STUDENT SERVICES is part of The Jossey-Bass
Higher and Adult Education Series and is published quarterly by Jossey-
Bass Inc., Publishers, 350 Sansome Street, San Francisco, California
94104-1310 (publication number USPS 449-070). Second-class postage
paid at San Francisco, California, and at additional mailing offices. POST-
MASTER: Send address changes to New Directions for Student Services,
Jossey-Bass Inc., Publishers, 350 Sansome Street, San Francisco, California
94104-1310.

SUBSCRIPTIONS for 1993 cost $47.00 for individuals and $62.00 for institutions, agencies, and libraries.

EDITORIAL CORRESPONDENCE should be sent to the Editor-in-Chief,
Margaret J. Barr, 633 Clark Street, 2-219, Evanston, Illinois 60208-1103.

Cover photograph by Wernher Krutein/PHOTOVAULT © 1990.

The paper used in this journal is acid-free and meets the strictest
guidelines in the United States for recycled paper (50 percent
recycled waste, including 10 percent post-consumer waste).
Manufactured in the United States of America.

CONTENTS

Editors' Notes

With the reduction of traditional sources of funding in institutions of higher education, student affairs is particularly vulnerable to budget cutbacks. Its role is often considered supportive and nonessential in comparison to academic affairs, which is perceived as primary and essential. Therefore, student affairs should consider alternative sources of funding.

There are a number of reasons for chief student affairs officers (CSAOs) to become involved in institutional advancement efforts. If CSAOs join the president and chief development officer in planning fundraising strategies, they are in a position to articulate the student affairs perspective in institutional goal setting and planning. Also, if they become involved in the solicitation process, they may become instrumental in the advancement effort. In addition, in the present climate, CSAOs with successful institutional advancement experience are more marketable.

However, there are reasons to eschew involvement in institutional advancement efforts. The time and energy of the CSAO and student affairs staff diverted to bringing in funding dilutes the programs and services provided to students. Also, some funding sources prescribe unreasonable program goals and time-consuming accountability requirements. In addition, staff hired to coordinate programs funded through external sources are eventually terminated when the external sources withdraw funding, thereby causing a number of personnel problems. Moreover, the CSAO may encounter resistance from the president and chief development officer when he or she attempts to become involved.

We believe that although there are problems associated with the involvement of student affairs professionals in institutional advancement, the benefits outweigh the risks. The purpose of this volume, *New Roles for Educational Fundraising and Institutional Advancement*, is to provide practical assistance in forming an effective strategy to enter the field of institutional advancement and educational fundraising.

There is confusion about the definition of terms associated with institutional advancement. It is common for the terms fundraising, development, university relations, public relations, and institutional advancement to be used interchangeably. However, in this volume, the terms are defined according to the guidelines outlined in the *Handbook of Institutional Advancement* (Rowland, 1986) and by the National Society of Fund Raising Executives. Institutional advancement is broadly defined as all of the programs and activities undertaken by a college or university to develop understanding and support from all of its publics for its education goals. This definition includes external and internal communications, government and public relations, educational fundraising, and alumni relations. Educational fundraising is defined as solicitation of gifts from private sources. It consists of four activities: annual giving, capital giving, deferred giving, and major gifts cultivation.

In Chapter One, Suzanne E. Gordon, Connie B. Strode, and Robert M. Brady explore the potential for creating communication networks between student affairs and institutional advancement within institutions as well as on regional levels. The relationship between and the fundraising roles of the CSAO and the chief development officer are explored by John E. Shay, Jr., in Chapter Two. In Chapter Three, Keith M. Miser and Teri D. Mathis present a guide to assist student affairs professionals in initiating successful fundraising programs targeted at alumni foundations, corporations, and parents. In Chapter Four, Laurence N. Smith offers a brief introduction to basic marketing principles to aid the student affairs professional in developing a marketing plan, conducting market research, and mobilizing and implementing an action plan. The findings of a survey of senior student affairs and development officers concerning levels of cooperation between the two functions and the degree of funding for student extracurricular activities are reported by Elaine C. Fygetakis and Jon C. Dalton in Chapter Five. In Chapter Six, Joe L. Davis and Sharon K. Davis discuss the results of a national survey of student affairs administrators. The findings provide insight into how institutional presidents regard the involvement of student affairs in grant-writing activities, institutional advancement activities, and organizational incentives. In Chapter Seven, Melvin C. Terrell, Donna E. Rudy, and Harold E. Cheatham present the findings of a survey designed to identify funding sources for minority student programming and to determine the implications in terms of institutional priorities. In Chapter Eight, the relationship between student affairs and advancement staff in mobilizing currently enrolled students to become future alumni donors is addressed by Robbie L. Nayman, Harry R. Gianneschi, and Judy M. Mandel through survey research findings. Based on an examination of the leadership role of CSAOs in regard to their institutional advancement activities and their role in strategic planning, James A. Gold, Dennis C. Golden, and Thomas J. Quatroche suggest, in Chapter Nine, that institutional advancement responsibilities should be integrated into the job descriptions of key student affairs staff.

In the concluding chapter, we present a summary of recommendations and an annotated bibliography of resource materials. It is our hope that this volume will help student affairs professionals become familiar enough with the field of institutional advancement to enter it in a fashion that increases their opportunities for success.

Melvin C. Terrell
James A. Gold
Editors

Reference

Rowland, A. W. (ed.). *Handbook of Institutional Advancement: A Modern Guide to Executive Management, Institutional Relations, Fund Raising, Alumni Administration, Government Relations, Publications, Periodicals, and Enrollment Management.* (2nd ed.) San Francisco: Jossey-Bass, 1986.

MELVIN C. TERRELL is vice president for student affairs and professor of counselor education at Northeastern Illinois University, Chicago.

JAMES A. GOLD is associate professor of educational foundations at the State University of New York College at Buffalo.

*The first critical step in creating a synergistic relationship between
student affairs and institutional advancement is to establish a dialogue
between the two units regarding educational fundraising activities.*

Student Affairs and Educational Fundraising: The First Critical Step

Suzanne E. Gordon, Connie B. Strode, Robert M. Brady

At a 1991 National Association of Student Personnel Administrators (NASPA)
conference interest session titled "Development and Fund Raising for Student Affairs," student affairs professionals from several campuses reported
phenomenal educational fundraising successes that occurred in cooperation
with their campus institutional advancement offices. Christine Wilkinson,
vice president for student affairs, and Lonnie Ostrom, director of development, at Arizona State University worked with their parents association to
develop a five-year institutional advancement plan. The first year, $130,000
was received to support student scholarships. In each of the following years,
between $140,000 and $180,000 was raised to designate rooms and to
purchase equipment for a new student services building, support tutoring
services, and support the library. In the fifth year, $200,000 was received
from the parents association to fund additional student scholarships. Initially, support from the Development Office included funding for a graduate
student. The second year, the salary for a full-time position was shared by
development and admissions, which is a part of the Division of Student
Services.

Keith Miser brought educational fundraising ideas and techniques with
him when he became vice president for student affairs at Colorado State
University. It did not take him long to begin a dialogue with the vice president
of development and external affairs. Money was reallocated from other
budgets to hire a full-time experienced institutional advancement officer
within student services. An aggressive program was designed, which would
pay for itself in three years and also raise additional funds for the division.
Parents, university vendors, and corporate and foundation support were

solicited. In the first year and a half, over $800,000 was secured in restricted gifts, primarily for scholarships, and an average of approximately $4,500 to $5,000 was received each month in unrestricted gifts for general use by the Division of Student Affairs.

What these cases have in common is the phenomenal success in raising funds for the division that the student affairs office can achieve when working with the institutional advancement office. These cases thus point to the urgent need for student affairs professionals to involve themselves in the business of educational fundraising. But how can this division, which is typically left out of the institutional advancement network, go about forging a link with those on campus whose function is "to devise and achieve the means that will provide the academic enterprise with needed resources" (Muller, 1977, p. 4)?

Such linkages are not typically in place at most institutions, so staff must create them. Because student affairs divisions should be primary benefactors of cooperative efforts with institutional advancement offices, we believe that student affairs professionals should take the first critical step: establish a dialogue with their institutional advancement office. While this may not be an easy task on many campuses, opening the lines of communication is the foremost prerequisite to action. Once these lines are open, both units can work together to maximize the benefits to the division as well as to the institution as a whole.

Organizational communications theory provides a useful framework for examining the conditions and means for establishing such a dialogue. In this chapter, we examine various methods for creating both formal and informal communication networks between the two units. None of this can be done without meeting some obstacles, however, so we next consider barriers that typically occur when new lines of communication begin to open and, specifically, how these barriers might be manifested in the context of student affairs and institutional advancement. Then, because none of the professionals in these two units functions in isolation from colleagues on other campuses, we conclude with a discussion of how to create communication networks between student affairs and institutional advancement on the regional and national levels.

As student affairs moves to legitimize its presence in the educational fundraising process, communication efforts both on and off campus can open the way to new and mutually rewarding relationships. But before this can happen, a change in how we view the structure of our higher education institutions may have to take place.

A Change in Perspective: Systems Theory

American colleges and universities typically are organized into structures that emphasize individually differentiated units and subunits (for example, academic affairs with its colleges and departments, student affairs with its various supportive programs). This differentiation within the institution represents, in part, both a set of values and a perspective on organizing. However, as the education environment becomes increasingly uncertain, this organizational strategy loses much of its usefulness.

In organizational theory, differentiation refers to "the differences in cognitive and emotional orientations among members of different units and the differences in formal structure among units" (Lawrence and Lorsch, 1967, p. 6). Integration, on the other hand, refers to the process of coordinating and linking departments or units within the organization.

The optimum organizational structure uses both differentiation and integration to fit the demands of the particular environment. When the environment is predictable, units are more effective if they place a greater emphasis on "formal rules and procedures [and] tighter spans of control" (Lorsch and Morse, 1974, p. 8). An uncertain external environment, however, requires a less formal internal structure and increased integration of units. Thus, as the environment changes from certainty (predictability) to uncertainty (rapid change), integration must increase.

Research reviewed by Rogers and Agarwala-Rogers (1976) explains why this is so. First, studies show that differentiated organizations have much slower rates of diffusion of innovations (new ideas, technology). Second, differentiated organizations have substantially lower overall productivity when individual units encounter tasks requiring collaboration with other units.

Consequently, we believe that future success requires an alternative perspective on organizational structure—one that seeks to establish new horizontal links within the university and to shape an integrated system of interdependent components. Such a perspective reflects the framework known as general systems theory (Bertalanffy, 1968; Boulding, 1965; Katz and Kahn, 1978). Systems theory "represents the organization as a complex set of interdependent parts that interact to adapt to a constantly changing environment in order to achieve its goals" (Kreps, 1990, p. 94). From this perspective, individual units are dependent on one another for optimal organizational functioning.

Certainly, the environment surrounding higher education at this time is one of rapid change. Equally apparent, institutions of higher education must adapt to this rapid change as quickly and effectively as possible in order to survive.

When we adopt a systems perspective, we see that colleges and universities are systems of interdependent units working together to achieve common goals. In systems theory, interaction among the units of the system produces synergy, where the combined and coordinated activities of the system create outputs that are more than the sum of the inputs alone. By working together, organizational units can do far more to achieve organizational goals than they can by operating alone.

Student affairs administrators can use this rationale to support their position for increasing the interaction between their unit and that of institutional advancement. The key to establishing this interaction is to remember that communication is one of the activities crucial for effective system functioning. As Katz and Kahn (1978, p. 223) suggested, "Communication—the exchange of information and the transmission of meaning—is the very essence of a social system or an organization." While communication occurs at various levels within any system, they see communication among units as a primary linking process. Through horizontal communications, units can ask for and share information relevant to their activities, thereby increasing coordination of activities.

This type of communication, and the systems perspective from which it derives, is already in use between the institutional advancement office and the academic units on most campuses. However, student affairs is seldom a part of this horizontal network. Yet, a direct link to the institutional advancement office would help both the student affairs divisions and the system as a whole to accomplish the institution's mission more efficiently and effectively. Toward that end, both formal and informal communication networks need to be established between student affairs and institutional advancement.

Establishing Communication Networks

Institutional advancement officers have several incentives for establishing relationships with student affairs. According to A. H. (Bud) Edwards (personal communication, January 25, 1993), vice chancellor for university advancement at the University of Arkansas, "Our business—the only reason we exist—is to raise private funds. Any time institutional advancement can set up relations with another institutional unit that has potential to bring in private funding, we're aggressive." He adds that since, historically, student affairs has not brought in private gifts, it can be a new funding source that will expand the capabilities of educational fundraising and benefit the institution. In addition, inclusion of student affairs in the educational fundraising network "gives us another advocate for what we can do. It's our opportunity to educate another unit on campus as to what educational fundraising does and can do."

As organizations attempt to cope with environmental uncertainty, the increased availability of horizontal communication channels (similar to "lateral relations" in Galbraith, 1977) fosters more information seeking and sharing. This increased flow of information then allows units to develop a common base of knowledge about one another's operation."

For example, it is likely that institutional advancement officers have only a cursory understanding of student affairs functions and little or no knowledge of the needs or objectives of that division. Since donors generally want to know how their donations will meet their needs and benefit the institution, it is vital that institutional advancement officers know specifically what the student affairs division does and why, what the division needs in order to function more effectively, and how the division's programs and services benefit the students and the institution as a whole.

Conversely, student affairs administrators need to know the language precepts of institutional advancement in general and the mission of the office on their campus in particular in order to provide appropriate information and assistance in raising funds for student affairs. For instance, institutional advancement offices normally accomplish their task of providing needed resources to their campuses through educational fundraising, securing of private corporate and foundation support, and alumni and public relations. According to Muller (1977, p. 8), one of the "basic ground rules" that govern successful institutional advancement is that the "pursuit of resources must fully interact with the use of resources." To help achieve such integration, several communication strategies are available.

Formal Lateral Contact Between Division Heads. Chief student affairs officers (CSAOs) can begin the dialogue with institutional advancement on their campuses in several ways. First, the CSAO can build a personal relationship of trust and respect with the chief institutional advancement officer through both formal and informal contacts. Formal contacts could include regular face-to-face meetings, periodic attendance at institutional advancement staff meetings, and participation in professional activities. Informal contact might be achieved through electronic mail, travel for educational fundraising purposes, social gatherings, pursuit of mutual interest, and seeking of advice. The overall goal is to understand each other as individuals, as professionals, and as private people; establish a consistent working style; use each other's time wisely; and share responsibility for the bottom line. The importance of this relationship in building the bond between institutional advancement and student affairs cannot be overstated—without it, other efforts have little chance for success.

Second, CSAOs can start to build the common base of knowledge referred to above so that each of the units comes to understand the other from the other's point of view. Discussion of the needs and strengths of student affairs with the chief institutional advancement officers and exploration of the institutional advancement's procedures and policies can lead to a more realistic assessment of likely problems and solutions and decrease defensiveness and misinformation.

Third, a CSAO can assign a staff person representing the division to work with the institutional advancement office and attend major staff meetings. There are several organizational models that can be followed for this purpose. For example, the staff person could be located in the student affairs division but report to institutional advancement. Or the person might both report to and be housed in either the institutional advancement office or a student affairs area. Shared salary arrangements can facilitate the acceptance of this person into both units.

Fourth, the CSAO can identify for the chief institutional advancement officer target areas that will lead to giving and identify the staff person heading each subunit to work with the staff person representing the division and the institutional advancement office. For example, the student affairs staff member might work with the director of orientation to target parents of new students; the director of campus activities, Greeks, and residence life to target student leaders; the director of financial aid to target scholarship recipients; the director of residence life and dining services to target vendors; or the dean of students to target alumni.

Weekly (or Monthly) Organizational Status Memos. Status memos are an excellent means of sharing information efficiently. To be useful to institutional advancement's purposes, they might include the following information: new programs and new needs within the division; names, addresses, and pertinent information for the potential donor list; reports of calls and contacts with foundations and corporations; and reports of specific efforts such as grant proposals, phon-a-thons, senior class gifts, and particular data bases.

Teams, Committees, or Task Forces Whose Goals Are to Discuss and Solve Interunit Problems. A solution that has become increasingly popular for dealing with resistance to change is to allow the people involved to participate in decision making and implementation of change. Resistance may result from blind spots and attitudes that staff have as a result of their preoccupation with their own area, or their inclination to accept stereotypes. For instance, "educational fund raisers are thought by some to be hustlers, beggars or high pressure salesmen" (Cheshire, 1977, p. 121). The practice of working together can help eliminate both tunnel vision and stereotypes.

Yearly Joint Conference. By sitting down away from day-to-day operations to discuss mission statements, goals, and objectives, the institutional advancement professional can better understand student affairs' needs and strengths, and the student affairs professional can better understand how institutional advancement builds a potential donor list and establishes relationships that lead to giving.

Boundary Spanners. Although the creation of multiple opportunities for communication can help to build a bridge between student affairs and institutional advancement, the use of boundary-spanning individuals also serves a crucial role in the establishment and success of horizontal communication. These individuals can function as formal or informal liaisons between units. For instance, Toffler (1970, p. 144) described the boundary spanners of the future when he suggested that "they will be skilled in understanding the jargon of different groups of specialists, and they will communicate across groups, translating and interpreting the language of one into the language of another."

There are two types of roles that boundary spanners can play: a formal managerial linking function with line authority (Galbraith, 1977) and an integrator function based on expertise without line authority (Pugh, 1979). For the lateral or integrator role to be effective, the person's knowledge of the organization and task must extend beyond his or her own specialization to include the operations and problems of both units. In addition to expertise in diverse areas, this person also needs stalwart communication skills to solve coordination problems.

Alternatively, when units experience intense disagreement over procedures or goals, a linking manager with line authority may be the only productive choice. We prefer the line authority manager hired by institutional advancement, paid on a 50-50 basis by institutional advancement and student affairs, and reporting directly to institutional advancement. This person should be a service-level operative, enthusiastic, aggressive, and knowledgeable about student affairs. He or she must be intimately involved in setting goals and objectives, designing the planning process, and setting up a data base of potential donors. The individual cannot function as a separate entity or be seen as competing for funds. Rather, he or she must carve out a new territory that incorporates the best of systems theory, creating interaction and interdependence for mutual benefit.

Although increased horizontal communication can be a positive goal, units must be on guard against "out-of-control" communication (Baird, 1977). This situation exists when managers who are frustrated with the delays of vertical communication increasingly shift their interaction to horizontal channels, which creates the potential for undermining channels of authority, losing control over the flow of information, and leaving upper-level management uninformed about actions at lower levels. Fayol (1949) anticipated this problem of balancing horizontal and vertical communications and proposed that each person who wishes to communicate across channels must first secure permission from his or her direct supervisor and each person who does engage in this communication activity must inform the supervisor about the outcomes of the interaction. The relevance of this proposal to the current discussion seems vital. Institutional advancement must have control over the process of approaching potential donors as well as the records of interaction with them.

Despite the contingency of an overzealous approach to the principles we are describing, both the formal and the informal communication channels described above offer a reasonable hope for establishing a mutually productive link between student affairs and institutional advancement.

Barriers to Integration

Although increased horizontal communication undoubtedly facilitates the work of integrating student affairs and institutional advancement, numerous organizational and individual barriers exist that can thwart such efforts. First, as Shay (this volume) points out, the approval of the president is necessary for inclusion of student affairs in institutional advancement planning. A skeptical president or a resistant board of trustees can create an insurmountable obstacle to student affairs involvement in educational fundraising activities. Consequently, CSAOs must prepare carefully to present their cases for inclusion in the best possible light. Use of the systems perspective and attention to Shay's recommendations should provide a sound basis for a positive decision by the president and subsequent approval by the board.

Second, as mentioned earlier, organizational units or staff often have stereotyped notions about others outside their boundaries of operation. Most of us have a natural tendency to evaluate and judge statements of other persons or groups, even when we have little firsthand knowledge of them. For instance, the student affairs division may be viewed as solely an administrative area, on the fringe of higher education and out of the educational fundraising arena. Institutional advancement offices need to know that student affairs divisions play a critical role in the academic missions of their institutions. The involvement of student affairs in enrollment management, retention, and student development is a potent element of the educational enterprise, on which institutional advancement can draw when approaching potential donors.

Third, organizational units vary in their willingness to share information with one another. Unwillingness may range from restricted communication to the use of misinformation. For example, the institutional advancement offices may be reticent to share information about educational fundraising efforts, which could be used by student affairs as models for planning. Conversely, student affairs professionals may not know what kinds of information institutional advancement needs to begin an educational fundraising effort and may decline to admit ignorance about how to approach potential donors, how much to ask for, and where and when to do this.

Fourth, due to organizational emphasis on differentiation and a unit's view of its own specialization, issues of "turf" or ownership may arise. For instance, colleges or departments recognize that there is a limited number of donors and that every entry into the field of educational fundraising means less for others. They may want to contact their own alumni, their own former student leaders, and the parents of their new students, feeling that donor lists would be duplicated by student affairs.

Fifth, divisions may not trust one another. This lack of trust may be justified, based on previous interactions where divisions competed for resources, or unjustified, based on the stereotypes described above. For example, if past educational fundraising activities by student affairs overlapped with institutional advancement efforts and a potential large donor either was lost because the individual was contacted by too many departments or gave a smaller gift because that was the first amount requested, a lack of trust may develop.

Knowledge of these barriers should not dissuade student affairs professionals from establishing a dialogue with institutional advancement. Rather, an advance understanding of potential obstacles can promote confidence and effectiveness in dealing with other units. Then, the experience of professionals on individual campuses may provide the impetus for extending the dialogue between student affairs and institutional advancement to the regional and national levels.

Regional and National Networks

Several professional associations provide management training for higher education administrators and may provide a base for creating regional and national communication networks between student affairs and institutional advancement. The primary organization for institutional advancement is the Council for the Advancement and Support of Education (CASE). Comparable student affairs organizations include NASPA, the American College Personnel Association, and the Southern Association of College Student Affairs (SACSA).

Currently CASE's core curriculum is very traditional and does not include any institutional advancement training for CSAOs. Only recently have they targeted the student recruitment and retention area. However, Richard A. Edwards (personal communication, June 25, 1992), senior vice president of professional services for CASE, has stated that "ensuring the future of our educational institutions is everyone's business—faculty, staff, alumni, and students. That means taking an active role in seeing that the institution receives adequate financial support for programs, people, and equipment. Student affairs officers can help to educate and mobilize students to be active supporters of their institution before and after they leave campus. As the national organization serving educational fundraising professionals, CASE is anxious to work with student affairs professionals to help them acquire the skills needed to become an effective part of the educational fund raising team." CASE has developed a program proposal outlining institutional advancement strategies for CSAOs, including the curriculum and suggestions for faculty. Several formats are suggested: an article in *CASE Currents,* a stand-alone regional workshop of three to five days, a preconference workshop attached to either a national or regional conference, a drive-in conference, and an interest session at a conference.

NASPA and SACSA have included interest sessions dealing with educational fundraising activities at their conferences, which met with standing-room-only participation. In addition, some CSAOs have reported attending the CASE workshop for academic deans, gaining relevant information and ideas. Thus, it appears that the time is right for establishing a dialogue between professional organizations to enhance and support efforts on individual campuses.

Conclusion

With the continuing and, in many cases, accelerating financial problems besetting higher education, educational fundraising will likely prove to be as important to student affairs as it has become to the academic divisions on our campuses. It may ultimately mean the difference between inadequate programming and effective student services. Consequently, student affairs officers must begin now to open the lines of communication with the institutional advancement office on their campus. This process will require time and sensitivity, a sense of purpose supported by a clear rationale, willingness to share information and to ask questions, awareness of anticipated obstacles and their impact on the process, and a certain amount of risk taking.

Organizational communication is frequently overlooked as a means of creating new relationships. However, its major principles can be used in a higher education setting to provide a rationale and framework to guide the establishment of new communication links between formerly disassociated units, such as student affairs and institutional advancement. Educational fundraising is, by definition, an activity that relies on effective communication. For student affairs professionals to tie into such activities, they must take the first critical step toward communicating the needs, strengths, and potential of their unit to those whose business is to raise funds.

References

Baird, J. E. *The Dynamics of Organizational Communication.* New York: HarperCollins, 1977.

Bertalanffy, L. V. *General Systems Theory: Foundations, Development, Applications.* New York: Braziller, 1968.

Boulding, K. "General Systems Theory: The Skeleton of Science." *Management Science,* 1965, 2, 197–208.

Cheshire, R. D. "The State of the Art." In A. W. Rowland (ed.), *Handbook of Institutional Advancement.* San Francisco: Jossey-Bass, 1977.

Fayol, H. *General and Industrial Management.* London: Pitman, 1949.

Galbraith, J. *Organization Design.* Reading, Mass.: Addison-Wesley, 1977.

Katz, D., and Kahn, R. *The Psychology of Organizations.* (2nd ed.) New York: Wiley, 1978.

Kreps, G. L. *Organization Communication: Theory and Practice.* (2nd ed.) White Plains, N.Y.: Longman, 1990.

Lawrence, P. R., and Lorsch, J. W. *Organization and Environment: Managing Differentiation and Integration.* Cambridge, Mass.: Harvard University Press, 1967.

Lorsch, J. W., and Morse, J. J. *Organizations and Their Members: A Contingency Approach.* New York: HarperCollins, 1974.

Muller, S. "The Definition and Philosophy of Institutional Advancement." In A. W. Rowland (ed.), *Handbook of Institutional Advancement.* San Francisco: Jossey-Bass, 1977.

Pugh, D. "Effective Coordination in Organizations." *S.A.M. Advanced Management Journal*, 1979, *44*, 29–35.

Rogers, E., and Agarwala-Rogers, R. *Communication in Organizations*. New York: Free Press, 1976.

Toffler, A. *Future Shock*. New York: Random House, 1970.

SUZANNE E. GORDON is associate vice chancellor for student services and dean of students at the University of Arkansas, Fayetteville.

CONNIE B. STRODE is a visiting assistant professor in higher education at the University of Arkansas, Fayetteville.

ROBERT M. BRADY is associate professor of communications at the University of Arkansas, Fayetteville.

This chapter explores, from the campus president's point of view, some of the potential pitfalls and major policy issues raised by engaging the student affairs staff in educational fundraising.

The President's Perspective on Student Affairs and Educational Fundraising

John E. Shay, Jr.

Few doubt that financial resources to support student affairs programs, already considerably restrained, will be squeezed even tighter in the foreseeable future. Rather than devote evermore creative energies toward simply making do with smaller slices of the institutional pie, many thoughtful chief student affairs officers (CSAOs) have concluded that they must increase the size of the pie, or, more accurately, the size of their slices, by raising external funds to support student affairs programs and activities. After all, difficult though it may be for the CSAO to apportion resources wisely across the student affairs spectrum, it is more agonizing to manage resource reductions in a manner that receives widespread acceptance, much less support. Far better, then, for the CSAO to find new sources of income from outside the institutional budget in order to maintain and even enhance student affairs operations.

Despite the obvious appeal of that strategy to alleviate serious budgetary pressures, the CSAO who resolves simply to charge out and ask prospective donors for money is making a serious, and possibly fatal, mistake. As with all other matters involving institutional policy, the wise executive should think through how the president and others might perceive the CSAO's direct involvement in institutional advancement. The CSAO may envision educational fundraising as a marvelous opportunity to increase the amount of external funds flowing to the institution as well as, personally, to become a more important institutional executive. The president, however, may view a move into institutional advancement as at best a diversion from the primary role of the CSAO and at worst a misguided incursion into someone else's area of responsibility.

NEW DIRECTIONS FOR STUDENT SERVICES, no. 63, Fall 1993 © Jossey-Bass Publishers

In this chapter, I provide insight into how the institution's chief fundraiser, the president, and other executive officers may view the active involvement of student affairs staff in raising funds from external sources. I also discuss major questions that the CSAO must address before embarking on an educational fundraising endeavor, touch base with a few of the major principles of educational fundraising, and comment on what portion of the student affairs program may or may not be appealing to prospective donors.

Context of Educational Fundraising

Once upon a time, according to higher education folklore, there were two kinds of colleges and universities: public and private. Because state support for public institutions covered virtually all of their operating expenses, state universities charged little or even no tuition to students. Private institutions relied on tuition payments and external support from alumni and friends to finance their operations. The distinction between public and private was obvious, particularly concerning the task of raising money from private sources.

Although the differences between public and private institutions were never quite that simplistic, today the distinctions have become so blurred that one can scarcely distinguish between the two. This is especially true in the case of institutional advancement. Most state-supported universities now employ large public relations and institutional advancement staffs to help create favorable institutional images and to raise huge amounts of money from nonpublic sources. Meanwhile, independent colleges and universities devote considerable attention toward obtaining federal or state support for their students, programs, or the institutions as a whole. Except for a handful of fiercely independent colleges, "private" institutions take all of the public support that they can get. Paradoxically, in many states the single biggest external educational fundraising operation by far is conducted by the flagship state university. Indeed, of the top twenty institutions in voluntary support in 1989–1990, eight were state universities ("Top Institutions in Voluntary Support," 1991).

Clearly, private educational fundraising is no longer restricted only to private institutions. Virtually every college and university, public or private, now considers external educational fundraising as an important vehicle for obtaining essential resources. Even community colleges, long the bastions of populist philosophy, are getting into the act.

The institutional advancement function has taken on extraordinary importance for nearly every college or university in recent years because other sources of income can no longer be relied on to cover the seemingly never-ending cost spiral. Enterprising CSAOs now seek to take matters into their own hands by raising money to support their own programs. Yet, doing so is not easy.

Division of Responsibilities. The division of responsibilities among major functional areas has a purpose. Financial affairs are so critical to institutional success as to require a chief financial officer with considerable expertise. Likewise, no president could get through the week without a senior academic officer to help handle relationships with the faculty and to provide oversight of academic programs. Most student affairs professionals are familiar with the long struggle to establish their field as a major area of responsibility rather than as just an adjunct to the academic programs.

Student affairs professionals, who rightly resent the unwarranted intrusion in decisions involving student social and educational issues by those primarily concerned about public relations or alumni reaction, ought to understand the institutional advancement staff's need to influence institutional advancement goals and control the educational fundraising process. Accordingly, one of the first moves that the entrepreneurial CSAO will want to make is to become an ally of the chief institutional advancement officer (CIAO). Any CSAO who plunges into educational fundraising without appropriate prior consultation is doomed to more than failure. Not only will the CIAO be outraged, but the president will be irritated, to put it mildly, by such an obvious overstepping of organizational bounds.

Major Donors. The CSAO must be aware that the student affairs staff's likely approach to educational fundraising—"We need money; wealthy people have money; let's ask them for it"—would cause dismay, to be kind, for both the president and the CIAO. This is especially so regarding contacts with prospective major donors.

Obtaining a major gift is a *process*, not an event. It entails thoughtful cultivation of contacts, usually over an extended period of time. It involves extended discussions to ascertain the donor's primary interests, as well as careful research to discover his or her financial capabilities. Those who think that careful coordination of solicitations is unnecessary should ponder the president's likely reaction to learning that the CSAO has just obtained a commitment of $10,000 from Mr. and Mrs. Moneybags to support the counseling center, when the president was about to ask them to consider contributing $1 million to endow a chair.

Donor relations at the major gift level are an intensely personal affair. On the one hand, the president does not want anyone to intrude unnecessarily or clumsily into the special relationship that most donors seek with the institution's chief executive. On the other hand, the president wants to extend donor relations to other key colleagues so that the donor's ties to the university transcend those of a personal relationship with the president. The CSAO who is truly an institutional executive, and not merely the senior administrator of the student affairs program, may be helpful in cultivating and ultimately soliciting targeted prospective donors.

Where to start? Let us look at the CSAO's involvement in educational fundraising, first, from the president's perspective and then from the perspectives of other institutional officers.

Presidential View

An adequate description of administrative relationships across the entire spectrum of American higher education requires a separate chapter, if not another book. Suffice it to say that although most presidents look upon the CSAO as an important institutional executive, they see the CSAO's primary involvement in terms of internal operations rather than external relations. As chief executive officer (CEO), the president concentrates more on the future and the external world than on day-to-day operations. If the institution has a separate chief operating officer, then the CSAO may report to that office rather than directly to the president.

Every CSAO must understand how the distinction between CEO and chief operating officer affects the president's view of student affairs, even if the president personally handles both portfolios. By merely raising the idea of educational fundraising, the CSAO will engage the attention of the president as CEO. The thoughtful CSAO, therefore, must explore, first, how she or he can help achieve the president's educational fundraising goals before exploring how to raise money for the student affairs program. Prior consideration of the president's goals is vital because his or her initial reaction will contain some or all of these questions: (1) Will involving the institution's executive officers in the educational fundraising process extend the president's reach to prospective donors, or will it cause confusion and dilute the donor's direct involvement with the president? (2) Helpful as it might seem in theory, will the CSAO's entry into educational fundraising constitute an unwise overlap and intrusion into the CIAO's domain? (3) Will the CSAO's involvement in educational fundraising divert attention away from his or her primary responsibility of managing the student affairs program? (4) Finally, although the CIAO may be the best, and certainly will be the most influential, person to answer this, are prospective donors likely to contribute significantly to support student affairs?

Other Institutional Executives. The involvement of institutional executive officers other than the CIAO in educational fundraising is a matter of style, not of just the president but also of the CIAO. Although in principle it makes sense to have several institutional executives interact meaningfully with prospective donors, some presidents and CIAOs prefer to handle the sensitive process of donor relations themselves. If this seems to be the case, the sophisticated CSAO must determine whether this practice reflects the president's (and the CIAO's) administrative philosophy or merely their conclusion that the current institutional executive officers lack the interpersonal skills necessary for effective donor relations. If the latter, it may seem awkward to involve only the CSAO in this activity. The CSAO should explore this matter with the president informally, and carefully, but only after first considering questions 2, 3, and 4 above.

Chief Academic Officer (CAO). The most likely executive colleague besides the CIAO to be involved in donor relations is the CAO. After all, much of the current educational fundraising program is in support of academic activities. Moreover, at the executive level, the CAO is often perceived as either second-in-command or first among equals. Persuading the president to involve the CSAO in educational fundraising when the CAO is not so engaged will be a tough sell, although not impossible.

Typically, the CAO's strength as a fundraiser flows not from skill in donor relations, although interpersonal skills are obviously helpful, but from his or her closeness to the academic program. The more knowledgeable and excited the CAO is about a department, a research project, or a faculty member, the more the prospective donor will be convinced that a contemplated gift will be truly worthwhile, and also deeply appreciated. While persuasiveness and other selling skills are clearly a bonus, most substantial donors become inspired when they come to share someone else's vision or dream. When a major commitment is sought, sincerity is more important than glibness.

Even though most donors perceive the university president as an educator, they recognize that she or he is also the institution's primary fundraiser. The CAO can add a dimension of academic legitimacy to any request for support of the academic program. And, obviously, most donors perceive the academic program as the heart of the institution.

Chief Financial Officer (CFO). Another potential, although not likely, participant in educational fundraising is the CFO. While late-night gab sessions at national student affairs meetings are replete with horror stories of atrocities committed by institutional CFOs, most presidents view their CFOs much more kindly. The president tends to give primacy to financial perspectives for many reasons, not the least of which is that institutional finances are usually a central concern of the governing board. Even though few presidents last long without a working knowledge of institutional finances, most rely on their CFOs for expertise in financial strategy.

Other institutional executives are sometimes perplexed by what appears to be a special bond between the president and the CFO. This can be true even if the two have very different, even contrasting, styles. This bond has nothing to do with personality and everything to do with function. While educators consume resources for important educational outcomes, financial officers focus their efforts on ensuring that the institution lives within its means. Frequently, this task requires the CFO to veto worthy activities for strictly financial reasons. The more unpopular the CFO's action may be among various constituencies across the university, the more grateful will the president likely be to the CFO for acting as a lightning rod; hence, the bond.

But the closeness between the president and the CFO transcends the role of taking the heat for unpopular decisions, important though that may be. The CFO is the only executive officer who shares the president's view that while the college or university is a distinctive kind of enterprise, it is still a business with a balance sheet. Educators need not, and perhaps should not, be concerned about the university as a business. But *somebody* must be, and that somebody is the CFO as well as the president.

What does all of this have to do with educational fundraising? Well, as the most businesslike officer in the university, the CFO is likely to be on the same wavelength as corporate executives and wealthy businessmen who are capable of making significant financial contributions. A knowledgeable CFO can convey to prospective donors a sense of confidence in the financial integrity of the institution. This confidence can be vital for institutions that are flirting with operating deficits, budgetary shortfalls, or other dark clouds.

Even if the CFO's personality relates well to potential donors, however, she or he is unlikely to be used heavily in solicitation because of the risk of sending a mixed message. The CFO's primary responsibility is fiscal account-ability: guardian of the expense side of the budget and custodian of the resources. To the extent that the CFO's educational fundraising involvement jeopardizes his or her reputation for stewardship, it is not worth the risk.

Centralization Versus Decentralization

The key to whether student affairs staff can or should engage in institutional advancement activities lies with the CIAO. The fundamental question is whether institutional educational fundraising is centralized or decentralized, which depends on both the size and scope of the institution as well as the CIAO's style and managerial philosophy.

Although some large universities maintain a centralized institutional advancement structure, the majority of those with several large specialized units, such as professional schools, teaching hospitals, and large athletic programs, decentralize most, but certainly not all, educational fundraising activities around logical units. At such institutions, a rational case can be made to organize a separate educational fundraising unit around student affairs. Where all educational fundraising is centralized, however, the CSAO will be hard-pressed to justify a separate educational fundraising activity for student affairs. In any event, the CIAO *must* play a major coordinating role, including veto power over proposed decentralized activities that may con-flict with universitywide goals. Those who pursue educational fundraising for student affairs are well advised to consult Desmond and Ryan (1985), Sandberg (1985), and Taylor (1985) in *CASE Currents,* the magazine of the Council for the Advancement and Support of Education, for a discussion of centralized versus decentralized educational fundraising.

What Is Institutional Advancement?

Perhaps this is an appropriate point to interject a few words about what is meant by institutional advancement. Only the naive believe that institutional advancement consists of two steps: (1) identifying sources of wealth and (2) asking them for money. Not only is that conception invalid, but just about the worst thing one can do immediately after identifying wealthy prospects is to ask them for money! Their most likely reaction to a premature solicitation will be either an outright rejection of the request or, sometimes worse, a token gift to make the solicitor go away.

Nor is institutional advancement the staging of events to which tickets are sold at a premium. Benefit events are a technique for raising relatively small amounts of money for small organizations or for specific targets. This tactic may be used as a starter for student affairs educational fundraising. Most professional institutional advancement officers, however, believe that the extraordinary efforts required to carry off an educational fundraising dinner or benefit performance can be better utilized in establishing a comprehensive program to identify prospective donors, to invite them to visit the campus regularly, to involve them in the life of the institution, and, ultimately, to solicit their investment in a particular program or the institution as a whole.

A description of what constitutes good institutional advancement practice transcends the purposes of this chapter. A brief computer search will uncover numerous books and articles about educational fundraising for colleges and universities. Any up-to-date institutional advancement officer should be able to recommend a number of publications on the field. One of the oldest, however, Seymour's (1988) *Designs for Fund Raising,* is still one of the best.

No matter how institutional advancement activities are organized, the wise CSAO should approach the CIAO to explore how student affairs can help achieve the institutional advancement goals of the university rather than how the institutional advancement staff can raise money for student affairs. This is not a tactic. It is common sense. The involvement of the student affairs division in supporting institutional priorities will educate the student affairs staff in the principles of sound educational fundraising, even as it generates confidence in student affairs among the institutional advancement staff.

Organize the Time. Even though educational fundraising may seem initially to be a better solution to the problem of constrained resources than is budget reduction, the CSAO must think carefully about how much time and energy can be reasonably devoted to institutional advancement. The CSAO's primary responsibility, after all, is to ensure that the entire student affairs program meets the appropriate needs of students within the context of the institution's mission.

Most presidents expect their CSAOs, first and foremost, to manage the student affairs divisions effectively and efficiently. Indeed, most CSAOs also see management as their primary responsibility. The question of how to incorporate institutional advancement activities into an already crowded schedule, therefore, merits careful consideration.

The CSAO must think about this question from the perspective of both his or her personal time as well as that of other staff members who may be called on for educational fundraising activities. The question of personal time is easier to resolve. Any experienced CSAO has developed a routine work schedule. Assuming that the go-ahead has been given for student affairs involvement in institutional advancement, the CSAO must decide how much time can be carved out for this activity. It is a good idea to discuss this with the CIAO, who can provide a general idea of the types of activities and the amount of time necessary to invest in a given educational fundraising enterprise. Which activities to postpone, reassign, or eliminate in order to engage in institutional advancement work will be a personal decision for each CSAO.

The more difficult task is to determine who else among the student affairs staff should participate in, and how much of their time should be allocated to, institutional advancement activities. This is where the rub comes. It is one thing to say that student affairs professionals should help raise money for student affairs programs. It is quite another to take them away from their primary responsibility toward students.

Presidential skepticism will be aroused by any plan that seems to remove people from their assigned responsibilities in order to work in another area. The CSAO should have a well-thought-out plan with identified limits on the amount of staff time devoted to institutional advancement, as well as a realistic explanation of how all current responsibilities will continue to be fulfilled.

Is Institutional Advancement Cost-Effective? Any CSAO who believes that educational fundraising is the answer to student affairs budgetary problems should first do a careful cost-benefit analysis to determine whether the effort expended is worth the revenue generated. This leads to the question of how much money can be raised from private sources to support the student affairs program.

Those inexperienced in educational fundraising often believe that donors are most likely to give where the need is greatest. If that were true, Harvard and Stanford would be in big trouble. Most donors want to support an exciting program rather than merely help an organization to stay afloat. Furthermore, donors are far more influenced by their own needs than by those of the institution. When it comes to the timing of a gift, the donor's needs prevail nearly all of the time. So, student affairs professionals may be in for a rude awakening if they presume that they can resolve this year's budget shortfall by asking wealthy people for money now.

Operating Support. Perhaps the most difficult problem for the CSAO, both in exercising professional judgment and explaining a prospective fundraising effort to the staff, is determining the marketability of student affairs programs and activities to prospective donors. This may come as a shock, but most people of means may have little initial interest in giving financial support to much, perhaps most, of the student affairs program.

Hardly anyone will give substantial sums to help an institution avoid reducing the size of either the staff or the operating budget. Why? Are prospective donors unable to see the value of ensuring adequate staff to meet student needs? The answer is that they can see the value of adequate staffing, but they view this problem as a continuing institutional responsibility, not as an attractive opportunity for philanthropy. Besides, most donors cannot afford the extraordinary sums required to pay for staffing.

We can say, poor Charlie's salary is only $30,000, and we ought to be able to raise that to keep him on board. Well, even ignoring the extra cost of fringe benefits, to retain Charlie as a permanent fixture will require contributions totaling $500,000, assuming a 6 percent payout rate on the investment. So, why not just raise a more modest $30,000 each year? Our friendly CIAO will be glad to tell us how many donors are eager to contribute to solving this year's budgetary problem with the certain knowledge that the same issue will be returning their way next year and for the foreseeable future. Donors want to build floodgates, not just plug holes in the dike.

Fundable Areas. Which areas are fundable? Student financial aid certainly is. Most universities have extensive scholarship programs supported by private donors. Many people of means derive satisfaction from the knowledge that they support deserving students. Helping others help themselves has a universal appeal.

The principles of market segmentation can help determine other areas that have educational fundraising appeal. To illustrate, although relatively few donors would leap to support "student activities," significant support can be generated for specific functions if we can identify alumni and others who are especially interested in the particular activities. Former members of the student union board, for example, might support a project that enhances the student union; former rugby players might support the rugby club; former staffers of the student newspaper, or perhaps the publisher of the nearest major newspaper, might be tempted to provide up-to-date equipment for today's student journalists. The elements needed are specific projects or activities and targeted groups of potential donors. Success requires both imagination to think of an appealing goal and a better set of records of former students' interests and activities than most institutions have available. Also needed are several interested alumni or other volunteers to help spearhead the educational fundraising drive.

All of this becomes very time-consuming, which is why the CSAO must make a cost-benefit analysis before embarking on educational fundraising as the answer to insufficient budgetary support for student affairs. It may well be that the prospective amounts generated are not worth the cost in staff time and energy used to raise the funds.

CSAO as an Executive

Different from the issue of raising money to support the student affairs program, however, is the role and stature of the CSAO as a college or university executive. Even presidents who are skeptical about raising funds for student affairs will appreciate having another administrative officer to help cultivate donors for broader university purposes. In this capacity, the CSAO becomes a part of a team, typically orchestrated by the CIAO, which takes a long-term view of raising friends and funds.

Indeed, adoption of a long-range view may be the best way for the CSAO ultimately to earn presidential endorsement for raising money for student affairs. Rather than ask what institutional advancement can do for student affairs, the wise CSAO first considers what student affairs can do for institutional advancement.

Involving Students. The student affairs staff are well positioned to help mobilize students to support institutional advancement events and activities. Whether as guides for campus tours, drivers for valet parking, or participants in a host of other activities to accommodate campus guests, well-scrubbed students can make a remarkably strong impression on prospective donors. After all, most donors see students as the ultimate beneficiaries of their largesse. Any CSAO who can deliver a continuing supply of bright, hard-working, and attractive students for assignment by the CIAO will earn the latter's gratitude and, doubtless, his or her support. The president will also notice.

At many institutions, direct student assistance to the institutional advancement program is already well established, but it has usually been initiated by the institutional advancement staff rather than by anyone in student affairs. Known generically as student alumni associations, their scope and potential are growing according to Fisher (1992), Olsen (1992), Ryan (1992), and Todd (1992). Even on campuses where student alumni associations are well developed, however, most CIAOs would welcome active involvement from student affairs staff in expanding the operations.

Recent Alumni. The CSAO can also help meet one of the CIAO's perpetual needs: converting newly minted graduates into contributing alumni. Although few people fresh out of college have substantial disposable incomes, getting recent graduates to contribute *any* amount to their alma mater is worth far more to the CIAO than the dollar amounts of their contributions. Establishment of the *habit* of giving is vital to a successful alumni program.

Typically, the individual amounts received from recent alumni are not great, but collectively they might support vital portions of the student affairs program. A "win-win" approach is for the CIAO to agree to allow student affairs to have first choice at soliciting recent alumni, that is, those who graduated no more than five or ten years previously. Recent alumni are more likely to support student affairs activities than to respond to generic institutionwide appeals. Meanwhile, the CIAO would be delighted to have a ready-made vehicle for maintaining contact with those who have established a continuing commitment to financial support. Even accurate, updated addresses are extraordinarily valuable to the CIAO. The specifics are not as important as the principle of working with the CIAO to address *institutional* goals, while generating extra support for student affairs. Such an approach is far more likely to generate presidential endorsement than is an effort focused solely on raising funds for the student affairs program.

Grants. The foregoing commentary has related primarily to solicitation from individuals and corporations. Foundation and government grants constitute another type of funding source. Although less anxious about contacts with foundations than with individual donors, the CIAO must nevertheless coordinate foundation approaches. Most foundations frown on multiple proposals from the same institution within a given time frame. The CSAO's best strategy is to develop a working relationship, either personally or through a staff designee, with the institutional advancement staff member who has primary responsibility for foundation relationships.

While most foundations pride themselves on their objectivity, in reality it helps to have an internal advocate. A good institutional advancement office is knowledgeable about the institution's network of contacts with individual foundations. Approaching a foundation with help from the inside is almost always preferable to mailing a proposal cold according to the foundation's guidelines.

Solicitation of government grants is far less likely to bruise internal administrative feelings than are other forms of seeking external support. The government grant award process is more focused and far more prescriptive than are the typical foundation's requirements. Assigning someone to scan the *Federal Register* for grant opportunities and maintaining sufficient communication to avoid competing proposals from within the same institution are the primary tasks. Usually, student affairs grant seekers need only follow the institution's general policy for obtaining government grants.

Summary and Conclusion

Successful educational fundraising is neither as simple as some suppose nor so mystical as to defy understanding. Any CSAO with good people skills can be a successful fundraiser, but skill should not be the CSAO's primary concern. The CSAO should first ascertain the president's philosophy on whether institutional advancement can or should be decentralized. Concurrently, the CSAO must enlist the CIAO as an ally, or at least as someone who will not erect roadblocks.

The personal involvement of the CSAO and the need for educational fundraising to support the student affairs program are two different questions. They may have different answers. If the president concludes that the CSAO can help with donor cultivation but that raising funds for student affairs programs is not a sufficiently high priority, the CSAO may have some tall explaining to do with the student affairs staff. Nevertheless, the long-term payoff for the entire student affairs program can be significant if the CSAO becomes well known among influential friends of the institution.

The most difficult decision for the CSAO, and one that the president will be pondering carefully, is whether the amount that can reasonably be raised from external sources can justify the extensive personal and staff energy required to raise it. In that regard, it is better to start small and build from the success of a few targeted projects than to create from scratch a comprehensive student affairs educational fundraising program.

One final observation is warranted. Successful educational fundraising can be an enjoyable and personally fulfilling enterprise, but it is also very hard work.

References

Desmond, R. L., and Ryan, J. S. "Serving People Needs." *CASE Currents*, 1985, *11* (3), 42–44.

Fisher, M. A. "Shining Examples." *CASE Currents*, 1992, *18* (5), 20–28.

Olsen, B. "SAAs: The Student's View." *CASE Currents*, 1992, *18* (5), 8–10.

Ryan, E. "Foundations for the Future." *CASE Currents*, 1992, *18* (5), 24–27.

Sandberg, J. R. "Organizing Your Operation." *CASE Currents*, 1985, *11* (3), 47–49.

Seymour, H. J. *Designs for Fund Raising.* (2nd ed.) Rockville, Md.: Fund Raising Institute, Taft Group, 1988.

Taylor, M. A. "Making Beautiful Music." *CASE Currents*, 1985, *11* (3), 50–52.

Todd, B. T. "SAAs: The Advisor's View." *CASE Currents*, 1992, *18* (5), 12–18.

"Top Institutions in Voluntary Support." *Chronicle of Higher Education,* Aug. 28, 1991, p. 36.

JOHN E. SHAY, JR., president of Marygrove College in Detroit, previously served as the chief student affairs officer at, successively, Marshall University, College of the Holy Cross, and the University of Rhode Island.

Choices about organizational design and leadership strategy must be made to create and implement an effective student affairs educational fundraising program. This chapter outlines a process that can be used to develop a successful program.

Creating a Student Affairs Institutional Advancement Program: Strategies for Success

Keith M. Miser, Teri D. Mathis

Across America, colleges and universities are facing reductions in public and private support for higher education. For the first time in decades, as this disturbing trend continues, many institutions have been forced to reduce their budgets. Programs are pared, eliminated, or reorganized, and student affairs programs often are included in this reduction process.

In response to shrinking institutional resources, student affairs programs are creating or enhancing institutional advancement programs specifically designed to raise funds for student affairs priorities. These gift dollars will replace lost institutional dollars, improve existing programs and services, or add new initiatives and programs.

In this chapter, we address the strategies needed to create and implement a successful student affairs institutional advancement program. The creation of institutional advancement programs for student affairs is a relatively new phenomenon. Even though much has been written about institutional advancement and educational fundraising, few references are specific to student affairs institutional advancement efforts.

Organizational Design

The structure and design of a successful institutional advancement program must be congruous with the overall institutional advancement plan. Two basic structures are common.

The first structure places student affairs institutional advancement within a centralized institutional advancement structure (Shea, 1986). In this model, the institution has a chief institutional advancement officer and a team of professionals who create and implement an institutionwide program designed to raise funds for all programs, such as scholarships, academic programs, endowed chairs, research, student affairs programs, the library, athletics, and capital projects. In this centralized mode, institutionwide priorities are set, case statements are developed, and educational fundraising resources are directed to these priorities. Often, in a centralized model, an institutional advancement officer works closely with each major institutional unit in the process of priority setting and needs assessment. It is imperative to have a liaison, advocate, or expert on student affairs on the central institutional advancement staff. This individual ensures that student affairs needs are articulated during priority setting and institutional advancement meetings with prospective funders. The liaison also should work closely with each student affairs program staff to gain knowledge and expertise on specific needs and priorities. Through this centralized process, a share of the funds raised is targeted to meet the needs of student affairs programs.

The second institutional advancement structure is the decentralized model (Shea, 1986), where each college, school, or program within an institution has an institutional advancement officer who coordinates the educational fundraising effort specific to that area. In many large and complex institutions, this model is long-standing and very successful; however, traditionally with this model, student affairs has not had an officer like those present in academic units. To implement this model, typically the chief student affairs officer creates the institutional advancement officer position, which is analogous to an institutional advancement officer in an academic unit. The ideal candidate is a midlevel professional with experience and training in both educational fundraising and student affairs.

The institutional advancement professional typically has an office within the senior student affairs office and is part of the central student affairs administrative staff. The institutional advancement officer should be included in the student affairs strategic planning process and meet regularly with program officers to fully understand and be sufficiently informed to articulate each area's vision, mission, needs, goals, and objectives.

This direct involvement ensures that the institutional advancement officer has the philosophical and operational understanding of student affairs necessary to articulate priorities, visions, and plans. Consequently, the institutional advancement officer with the chief staff can set priorities and develop appropriate educational fundraising strategies for the division. From this structural base, a unique, energetic, and forceful program can be developed.

Leadership Strategies

To have a successful institutional advancement program, leaders at many organizational levels must support and be involved in the effort. The institution's president must be confident that an institutional advancement program, focused on the needs of student affairs, is in the best interest of the institution. This support is critical because the president influences or sets institutional priorities for educational fundraising. As a student affairs institutional advancement program matures, the president often is involved with potential individual donors, corporate and business leaders, and constituent groups who are being cultivated for gifts based on student affairs priorities. An institutional advancement program cannot be successful without the active involvement of the president (Pray, 1981).

The chief student affairs officer is the primary leader who moves the program from its inception to an active, viable, and successful venture. This leader manages the division's strategic planning and goal setting and sets the key priorities for the institutional advancement effort. The chief student affairs officer also is involved deeply in the cultivation and solicitation of major donors.

In the early stages of the institutional advancement program, the chief student affairs officer must lead, support, and inspire the educational fundraising effort, because the work is difficult and the early returns are small. Many staff members may be skeptical about the emerging institutional advancement program, especially about the initial costs compared to the returns, at a time of scarce resources. In response, the chief student affairs officer must be positive, forward-looking, and willing to take short-term risks for long-term gains.

A key initial task for the institutional advancement officer is to "teach" the division's entire professional staff how the institutional advancement process works and clarify the elements, roles, and strategies required for an excellent program. Together, they must discuss process, goals, roles, ethics, stewardship, and philosophy. Staff members must learn about principles such as deferred giving (gifts made through trusts, bequests, life insurance, and other methods where the gift is planned now but its use by the organization is deferred until after the death of the donor), donor intent (how the donor wants his or her gift to be used), and restricted and unrestricted gifts (gifts that may or may not be limited to a specific purpose), as well as about cultivation (creating and maintaining relationships with current and potential donors to the organization), proposal writing, and legal issues. The institutional advancement officer then must help specific department chairs or program directors define and articulate needs, write case statements, and develop proposals. In general, this professional must direct the process and manage the program from the first ideas through gift registration and acknowledgment. In addition, the institutional advancement officer must coach the chief student affairs officer and the president, while continually planning and actively moving all aspects of the program forward successfully.

The department chairs or program directors and their staffs play a vital role by identifying needs, writing case statements and expressions, designing programs, and assisting in cultivation and solicitation. It is important to remember that in the early stages, program leaders often are skeptical. They feel that they do not have the time to be actively involved, and at times they are critical of the funding needed to initiate an institutional advancement effort, when those funds could directly support their individual programs.

Student leaders can and must play a role as the program matures. They can be invaluable in the cultivation and solicitation of potential donors. Prospective donors to education, whether parents, alumni (Miller, 1986), corporate leaders, or foundation representatives, have one thing in common—they support students. Used properly, student involvement is a vital ingredient as well as a great asset in a successful educational fundraising program.

Leadership and Communication

One of the critical principles in any successful institutional advancement program is open and frequent communication among all involved. The chief student affairs officer and the institutional advancement officer must meet often to coordinate efforts. Also they must keep the president informed and involved as well as provide a frequent and consistent information flow to the student affairs program directors to enhance their support of and involvement in the program. Moreover, a series of strategies must be developed to communicate to donors and potential donors on both formal and informal bases, through cultivation activities and case expressions.

The chief student affairs officer, the institutional advancement officers, and the program directors must continuously develop support inside the institution's organizational framework, with the chief student affairs officer assuming the paramount leadership position. This central leadership role is essential to elicit the support and assistance of other institutional leaders such as deans, department chairs, faculty, and the president. It also is necessary, as an ongoing effort, to teach the campus about the vision and goals of the division of student affairs and the necessity of keeping these goals high on the list of the institution's priorities to serve students, parents, and other constituents. Without this constant effort, student affairs priorities will likely be lost among other pressing institutional needs.

Educational Fundraising Process

Before a successful educational fundraising program can be established to meet divisional goals, those needs and goals must be incorporated into the institution's priorities. Ideally, student affairs' goals will be identified as encompassing high institutional priorities, thus increasing the ability of the institutional advancement office to pursue and successfully obtain private contributions restricted to those purposes (Brittingham and Pezzullo, 1990). As soon as a vision and a priority level have been assigned to the student affairs institutional advancement effort, the staff can prepare a case statement.

Developing the Case Statement. The internal case statement encompasses all of the reasons to support an organization. It answers the questions "Why?" and "What for?" This document, compiled from existing resources, is based on institutional traditions. The statement articulates why the institution exists, whom it serves, what needs it fulfills, why its work is important, how it is distinctive, what are the short- and long-term needs, why the institution will be successful in carrying out its plans, who is associated with the organization, and who should support the institution (Wagner, 1991).

The resulting document should be comprehensive, focusing on more than one college or division (Pray, 1981). From this internal case statement come the external case expressions (Wagner, 1991). These documents distill information from the big picture and present it to the institution's constituents in a clear and compelling format.

Case expressions may take the form of brochures, letters, articles, speeches, press releases, or prospectuses. They may highlight any single need or collection of needs. Always, a case expression tells a prospective donor how to give.

The division of student affairs must develop its own case for giving. The case statement must be available in a written format and should clarify how the division works within the institutional framework to achieve goals that benefit society. It should tell the prospective donor exactly why a contribution to the division is important and what that gift will accomplish. The case statement and case expressions are the sales tools that inspire participation and, as Pickett's (1977) research suggests, are central to educational fundraising success.

To illustrate, an abbreviated case statement for an educational program might include the following: "Three complex societal issues currently impact the business climate in the United States: the emergence of a global economy, the increase in diversity in the general population, and the rapid growth of technology and technology transfer opportunities. The [institution's name] Division of Student Affairs is rapidly becoming a national leader in the development of programming that addresses these issues." The case statement would then go on to outline the programs that meet these challenges and why private support is necessary to continue and expand the work of the division. It would also indicate how the programs listed work as part of the overall university mission.

Who Are the Potential Donors? Several issues should be addressed when considering who will be approached to contribute to the division: Is the constituency linked in any way to the division? Is this constituency interested in the division's programs and activities? Is this constituency able to make contributions to the division? Is this constituency already on the institution's prospective or current donor data base?

If the first three questions can be answered affirmatively, then the final consideration is vitally important. If the constituency or individual prospect already is targeted within an educational fundraising strategy of a unit or the institution as a whole, then a solicitation must be coordinated within the overall institutional advancement effort or postponed until an appropriate tactic is determined. When establishing an educational fundraising program, it may be propitious to identify a constituency that is not currently solicited for other institutional programs and determine whether there are affirmative answers to the first three questions listed above. All ongoing solicitation efforts to benefit student affairs then can be coordinated through the central institutional advancement office.

Matching Divisional Needs and Donor Interests. Consider the level of the match between a prospect's interests and the division's case. The more closely the division's goals are related to a prospect's reason for giving, the more likely it is that funding will be forthcoming (Read, 1986).

Different funding sources give for different reasons. By far, the most money is contributed by individuals (Van Til, 1990, p. 46). However, the concept of "giving to charity" is yielding to the idea of philanthropic investment (Brittingham and Pezzullo, 1990; Lord, 1983). Student affairs programs have been very successful in finding solutions to problems in education. Promote those successes and the objectives and ideas of the division to individuals and allow them to invest in the institution's success (Broce, 1986).

Corporations are committed to making thoughtful contributions according to enlightened self-interest (Van Til, 1990). Success in finding a match between the division and a corporation involves understanding company goals and determining how programs within student affairs can assist corporations in meeting those goals. Appropriate matches may include programs that target the recruitment and retention of individuals from minority backgrounds; these programs appeal to corporations concerned with the demographics of their future work forces.

Philanthropic foundations are established with the intent of giving money to appropriate causes; however, requests vastly outnumber the level of funding available. Less than 7 percent of all requests receive funding (Read, 1986, p. 27). Again, the more closely a program matches a foundation's interests and geographical scope, the greater the likelihood of success in the fundraising effort.

Prospect Research. Many institutions have resources to assist with the identification and research of prospects. Determine whether a research office exists within the institutional advancement division and what services may be available to student affairs. In addition, resource books that identify the interests and guidelines of corporations and foundations are available in most institutional and public libraries.

Information about individuals is obtained most easily through a research office with access to clipping services and extensive long-term files. Check with the office of institutional advancement first. Some of the most timely information about individuals is anecdotal and can be retrieved from other student affairs professionals, who may meet the prospects. For example, residence hall directors may be aware of which students come from backgrounds of wealth or which parents show significant interest in the campus.

Donor Pyramid. Most top funding sources are already identified by an institution, and ongoing strategies are in place to solicit major gifts. The challenge for fundraisers and for those who are attempting to initiate new programs is to find, cultivate, and solicit prospects with the potential to give significant gifts. The good news is that there are more individuals with this potential than ever before, and many of them are not currently being solicited (Nichols, 1990).

Conventional wisdom proclaims that 10 percent of all donors provide 90 percent of all philanthropic dollars (Brossman, 1981, p. 69; Lord, 1983, p. 47). However, new demographic trends show that this donor pyramid is narrowing, with 5 percent of contributors donating 95 percent of all gifts (Nichols, 1990, p. 15). According to Nichols (1990), this means that there is greater potential in the middle sector and continued stability in the bottom of the pyramid.

Annual Fund. Although the majority of the funds that a division can raise will eventually come from a few donors, an annual giving program provides a source of stability through receipt of ongoing, current dollars. It is an organized, recurring effort to solicit donations for the needs of an institution or division (Williams, 1981, p. 5). The annual fund also serves as a vital step in the cultivation process.

The annual fund is a broad-based appeal directed toward targeted constituencies, such as alumni or parents, who have links to the division but may have no prior giving history. During the activities of an annual fund, new donors are obtained and previous donors are renewed or persuaded to make larger gifts. The goal of the annual fund is to provide resources that help to meet the most urgent needs of the division and that can be renewed and expanded each year.

Most of the gifts received during an annual drive are below the level of major gifts. Each institution defines these levels somewhat differently. The institutional advancement office can provide this information. Annual gifts are a way for a constituent to get to know the institution and to demonstrate current support. Hopefully, this support will continue and increase over time. Nichols (1990, p. 151) observed that once a prospect indicates an interest in the division's programs by sending that first check, then "the organization steps up communication, hoping to acquire, speedily, a second gift, and a new, committed donor." Some of the donors acquired through the annual fund become the major donor prospects of the future.

Cultivation and Solicitation. Regardless of the level, each prospective donor undergoes all or part of the cultivation cycle. Steps in this cycle include identifying prospects, dispensing information, creating awareness and then knowledge, developing interest and involvement, and encouraging investment. Cultivation may be as simple as receiving information about the division through a letter, brochure, or newsletter or attending a campus event. Cultivation also can mean an organized strategy to build linkages through invitations to events, volunteer activities, telephone and mail contacts, personal visits, and board assignments. The stages of cultivation have a variety of effects, depending on the institution's goals (Jacobson, 1986, p. 20). The goal of cultivation activity in educational fundraising is to develop the prospect's interest, involvement, and commitment to making a gift.

The cultivation cycle is an ongoing process that includes promotion of good relationships with donors. Many institutions have offices of donor relations or gift acknowledgment processes to assist the division in recognizing the generosity of its donors. Contact the institutional advancement office to determine what services are available.

Model Program

The mission statement for the Office of Development for Student Affairs at Colorado State University (CSU) outlined the following goals: (1) develop an annual giving program to meet the unrestricted needs of the division, (2) institute a parents program as the foundation for annual and major giving, and (3) establish a corporate and foundation relations program to help fund the division's priority projects.

Constituency Identification and Data Base Collection. Student affairs' first challenge in educational fundraising at CSU was to identify a constituency not currently solicited by an existing program. Academic colleges solicit their alumni, but parents had never been contacted, except to pay tuition and parking tickets. Student affairs arranged with the Office of University Development to have current parents assigned to the division as its principal constituency. The rationale was that student affairs programs benefit all students throughout their tenure at the university, regardless of their academic discipline.

The Office of Admissions and Records collects and updates the data base. Labels and personalized letters can be printed by this office, or a magnetic tape can be made of the data so that the Office of Development can handle production. The Office of Admissions and Records also updates the data base to indicate which students have left the university and which parents have changed their addresses. The parent address fields are protected so that students cannot make changes without confirmation from the parents.

Other constituencies that may be underutilized at an institution include alumni who worked as student paraprofessionals, were student leaders, or participated in student government; local business people who rely on student patronage; and grandparents of current students. It is important to consider the potential of such groups when developing constituencies for student affairs.

Cultivation. At CSU, parents are initially approached through a newsletter, titled "Writing Home." Although this vehicle serves primarily as an information and cultivation conduit to parents, an institutional advancement message is included in each issue as well as a response device for contributions. Donations received as a direct result of the newsletter more than cover the cost of the program, and the program helps the division acquire first-time donors. One issue each year is dedicated to an honor roll of parent donors.

Some programs established in the last two years to enhance linkages with parents include expanded activities during Family Weekend and a complete track of informational sessions for parents during student orientation. At each event, interaction between parents and student affairs professionals is stressed, and the services and programs that benefit students throughout their tenure at CSU are highlighted.

Solicitation. The newsletter, along with two mailed solicitation pieces each year, are the division's case expressions and comprise the foundation of the division's annual fund. Future plans for expansion of the annual fund include fall and spring phon-a-thons to parents who now are aware of the needs of the division and are interested in the institution. The number of parent donors is increasing steadily, and a dramatic jump is expected as the updated data base allows personal contact with parents through the telemarketing program.

Student volunteers recruited from fraternities and sororities will facilitate the fall telemarketing campaign. The spring phon-a-thon will be targeted to those who did not respond to the fall and winter solicitations and will be conducted by the Office of University Development.

Some major donor prospects have been identified through parent mailings and activities. These prospects have been incorporated into a cultivation strategy that ultimately will place them in contact with either the vice president for student affairs or the president for personal solicitation. This strategy, as well as the solicitation, will be orchestrated by the Office of University Development.

Corporate and Foundation Prospects. The second aspect of the annual giving program focuses on those corporations and businesses with whom CSU has strong links but who have never been solicited: vendors. Any business that had done business with the university was reviewed. Those who had a record of providing goods or services in excess of $50,000 were targeted for solicitation. The Office of Development for Student Affairs produced a newsletter that promoted the need for corporate involvement in student affairs, recognized those who had made contributions to the division, and discussed the economic impact of both the division and the university on the geographical region. Following the newsletter mailing, personalized solicitation letters were sent, followed by personal calls from students and volunteers.

Future Expansion. Those constituencies already under development will be tracked and encouraged to make regular gifts to the division through a variety of direct-mail strategies, telemarketing programs, special events, and personal cultivation and solicitation. The result of regular contact with these prospect pools should be a steady increase in annual contributions through renewals and new donations. As donors are identified and cultivated, they will be encouraged to move the donor pyramid to higher levels of support.

Corporations and foundations will be cultivated to determine interests so that appropriate matches are made within the division. Development staff and the vice president for student affairs will continue to teach program directors how to respond directly and appropriately to requests for proposals, which in turn expedites the educational fundraising process.

Through careful management, a strong donor base will be built to ensure the division's ability to respond to future needs and opportunities. From that base will come the major gifts that will not only support the division in the future but also create a strong foundation for today.

Summary

This chapter has identified specific processes, strategies, and models that can be used to create, plan, implement, and administer a successful student affairs institutional advancement program. A critical first step is to select an organizational design that is congruous with the financial needs and culture of the institution. This design can be built on a centralized or decentralized model. Leadership and communication are central to any successful program, and the chief student affairs officer must play a major role by providing overall direction, marshaling resources, and ensuring that the educational fundraising goals parallel the priorities in the division of student affairs. This leader also is responsible for keeping the president informed at all times as well as involved at key points in the educational fundraising process.

An overview of the educational fundraising process was presented, starting with the development of a case statement designed to clearly articulate the division's needs and, in turn, to support the identification and cultivation of potential donors. Donor research and cultivation are important steps in this process of matching the goals of the program with the interests of the potential donor.

This initial process can be used at a time when adequate funding is a critical issue at most institutions and for nearly all student affairs programs. A successful and vital program can be built on the principles and strategies detailed here, which allow student affairs to create a strong educational fundraising program on a foundation shaped to emphasize institutional strengths and program distinctiveness.

References

Brittingham, B. E., and Pezzullo, T. R. *The Campus Green: Fund Raising in Higher Education.* ASHE-ERIC Higher Education Reports, no. 1. Washington, D.C.: Association for the Study of Higher Education, 1990.

Broce, E. *Fund Raising: The Guide to Raising Money from Private Sources.* (2nd ed.) Norman: University of Oklahoma Press, 1986.

Brossman, W. R. "The Central Importance of Large Gifts." In F. C. Pray (ed.), *Handbook for Educational Fund Raising: A Guide to Successful Principles and Practices for Colleges, Universities, and Schools.* San Francisco: Jossey-Bass, 1981.

Jacobson, H. K. "Skills and Criteria for Managerial Effectiveness." In A. W. Rowland (ed.), *Handbook of Institutional Advancement.* (2nd ed.) San Francisco: Jossey-Bass, 1986.

Lord, J. G. *The Raising of Money.* Cleveland: Third Sector Press, 1983.

Miller, J. H. "Communicating with Alumni." In A. W. Rowland (ed.), *Handbook of Institutional Advancement.* (2nd ed.) San Francisco: Jossey-Bass, 1986.

Nichols, J. E. *Changing Demographics: Fund Raising in the 1990s.* Chicago: Bonus Books, 1990.

Pickett, W. L. "An Assessment of the Effectiveness of Fund-Raising Policies of Private Undergraduate Colleges." Unpublished doctoral dissertation, Department of Education, University of Denver, 1977.

Pray, F. C. "The Case Statement as Development Tool." In F. C. Pray (ed.), *Handbook for Educational Fund Raising: A Guide to Successful Principles and Practices for Colleges, Universities, and Schools.* San Francisco: Jossey-Bass, 1981.

Read, P. E. *Foundation Fundamentals.* New York: Foundation Center, 1986.

Shea, J. M. "Organizational Issues in Designing Advancement Programs." In A. W. Rowland (ed.), *Handbook of Institutional Advancement.* (2nd ed.) San Francisco: Jossey-Bass, 1986.

Van Til, J. "Defining Philanthropy." In J. Van Til and Associates, *Critical Issues in American Philanthropy: Strengthening Theory and Practice.* San Francisco: Jossey-Bass, 1990.

Wagner, L. (ed.). *Principles, Techniques of Fund Raising.* Indianapolis, Ind.: Fund Raising School, 1991.

Williams, M. J. *The FRI Annual Giving Book.* Rockville, Md.: Fund Raising Institute, 1981.

KEITH M. MISER is vice president for student affairs at Colorado State University, Fort Collins.

TERI D. MATHIS is associate vice president for annual giving, University of Colorado, Boulder.

Marketing provides student affairs professionals with some of the most effective strategies, techniques, and actions for success. This chapter, written for professionals without a marketing background, provides a design for the development of a strategic marketing approach to educational fundraising.

Marketing: A Key Ingredient for Educational Fundraising Success

Laurence N. Smith

The integration of marketing concepts into professional work in student affairs is immensely beneficial. Although this chapter's focus is on how marketing can assist in educational fundraising, the strategies and tools can also be utilized by the student affairs professional to convert mission into action, to provide effective and efficient use of limited human and support resources, and to attain the objectives of various student affairs programs, services, and activities. Furthermore, marketing can help student affairs staff achieve desired outcomes such as attraction and retention of new students, increased attendance at social events, increased faculty and staff involvement in programs, and effective targeting of students in need of counseling, alcohol and drug education, tutoring, or special assistance.

The usefulness of marketing techniques and concepts is obvious as they are applied to the tasks of attaining desirable tangible outcomes such as the number of students enrolled, residence hall occupancy, food service contracts sold, or ticket sales for campus concerts and athletic events. But the application of marketing techniques to intangibles such as ideas and services to achieve desired outcomes of school spirit, goodwill, and customer satisfaction is also possible, even though the outcomes are more difficult to define and measure.

In 1985, the American Marketing Association issued a broadened definition of marketing: "The process of planning and executing the conception, pricing, promotion, and distribution of ideas, goods and services to create exchanges that satisfy individual and organizational objectives" ("AMA Board Approves New Marketing Definition," 1985). The key concept in the marketing definition is the exchange process: activities associated with two or more parties giving something of value to each other that satisfies their perceived needs. Marketing pertains to how we create or influence these exchanges (Kotler and Andreasen, 1991, p. 71).

Educational fundraising is an exchange process. Since it more often than not deals with intangibles such as how we identify and satisfy donor needs, there is a direct link to the marketing process. The role of the student affairs professional as fundraiser, then, is initially one of focusing on the needs of the individual, organization, foundation, or agency to be solicited in an effort to create an exchange process with the college or university. Therefore, student affairs professionals will be successful only if they fully understand the prospective donors' needs, and what triggers those needs, and then determine how the needs can best be met by their institutions and respond accordingly.

Regardless of the fundraiser's level of sophistication in marketing, the development of a strategic marketing educational fundraising plan is the critical starting point for integrating marketing applications into the educational fundraising process. The strategic marketing plan helps student affairs professionals develop a clear understanding of the efforts and level of involvement needed, and it provides a framework to identify and resolve relevant marketing issues. The planning process also ensures that the support resources necessary for success are identified before the fundraising process begins and that their role in achieving the desired educational fundraising outcomes is understood. The planning process is also important because, if properly executed, it will develop throughout the student affairs division an understanding of and support for the educational fundraising initiative. This understanding is a key ingredient of success since individuals tend to support what they help to create.

The commitment by student affairs professionals to participate in educational fundraising should be rooted in a thorough understanding of what educational fundraising entails and should be made in two stages. The first stage is to commit to developing a strategic marketing educational fundraising plan. The second stage, once the plan is fully developed, is to determine the degree of support for the plan from the division and administration and then whether or not, and how, to proceed. One must then either agree to use the plan as formulated or else modify it prior to its implementation. But it is always critical to keep in mind that the foundation for success is a strategic marketing educational fundraising plan.

Developing a Strategic Marketing Educational Fundraising Plan

A strategic marketing educational fundraising plan consists of the following elements: executive summary, goals, situation analysis, strategies, resources, operations, evaluation and renewal, and appendixes. Each of these elements is described in greater detail below.

Executive Summary. The executive summary is written after the total report has been completed; the summary is placed at the front of the plan. It is intended to serve as a one-minute, prime-time commercial and should be written accordingly. It contains the main elements of the strategic marketing educational fundraising plan (briefly stated) that are important to the reader regardless of whether the rest of the report is examined.

Goals. What educational fundraising outcomes are desired? Goals are best stated in clear and concise end-results terms and should be realistic, measurable, and time-bounded.

Situation Analysis. This section describes where the university and student affairs division are in relation to achieving the goals. Other key elements in the situation analysis are an examination of internal and external forces that confront the institution, a brief historical overview, identification of the mission and how the institutional advancement goals help to achieve it, an overview of the institution's current advancement efforts and the assumptions that guide them, donor giving patterns, cultivation and conversion activities, and a statement about competition and market share.

There should also be an explanation of the marketing mix, commonly referred to as the "four p's" of marketing: (1) *product* (conception or offer): what the educational fundraising effort is providing to donors; (2) *price:* what the tangible and intangible costs are to donors; (3) *place* (distribution): how individuals become donors, what offices they have to work through and their locations, and how the offices reach out, either through home or office visits with prospective donors, attorneys, accountants, and so on; and (4) *promotion:* what message is communicated to donors and how it is communicated (letters, brochures, video- or audiotapes, advertising in electronic or print media, direct mail, personal visits, telephone contacts, or special events). Promotion also includes how the communications and offers are packaged, the graphic designs used, and the incentives offered to encourage the exchange. Promotion is intended to create attention to and awareness and understanding of the offer, which in turn, if the effort is successful, lead to gifts, grants, or awards to the institution. The situation analysis should also include information about current educational fundraising management capabilities, as well as the human and support resources available for the institutional advancement effort both within the institution at-large and, in particular, within the division of student affairs.

The situation analysis closes with an analysis of the information presented, and identification and discussion of the strengths and weaknesses of current educational fundraising efforts. Finally, brief recommendations are offered about how the educational fundraising should proceed in light of the analysis and discussion.

Strategies. Strategies are miniplans outlining how to achieve the goals. The main areas of strategy development are segmentation and targets, positioning, product, price, place (distribution), and promotion.

The process of generating strategies should involve many individuals, since creativity is stimulated by the sharing of multiple perspectives. Those who should be involved include student affairs colleagues, institutional advancement professionals, students, parents, faculty, and alumni.

A think tank concept characterizes the most successful approach. Participants from the above-named groups are invited to meet as consultants to the process of formulating a strategic marketing educational fundraising plan. Once they are informed of the goals and objectives and presented with highlights from the situation analysis, they can help identify strategies for each of the areas described below.

By letting participants know in advance that their ideas are needed and that the consulting sessions will be fast-paced and interactive, enthusiastic supporters can be attracted who are willing to spread the message and help with the educational fundraising effort. The think tank process generates numerous strategies, ideas, and suggestions that enrich, expand, and refine the institution's thinking and planning. The think tank also serves as a foundation for implementation of the plan as it creates a strong basis for involvement in the initial stages of the educational fundraising process. This pays off in later stages when staff members are solicited to make a gift or are asked to solicit others. This approach gives further meaning to the concept that people support what they help to create.

Segmentation and Targets. A segment is a heterogeneous group with similar needs or levels of responsiveness to what is offered. A target is a homogeneously grouped subset within the segment to whom the educational fundraising efforts will be directed. The following broad categories are the segments on which educational fundraising efforts should focus: individuals, organizations, foundations, and agencies and corporations.

Individuals include students, parents, alumni, and friends. The difficulty in dealing with a segment as a whole, or even a subsegment, is whom to contact. The number of people is very large, and thus it is both expensive and difficult to communicate with all of them. Targeting provides the opportunity to reach individuals who are most likely to respond, as well as the opportunity to test a sample within the target to see if either hunches or research findings are on track.

Targeting of the potential donor base, therefore, is a critical step. One strategy might be to target only those individuals who currently have or in the past had a strong involvement with the program. For example, these might include parents of students who receive scholarships or alumni who worked as resident advisers or held elected student government positions.

Knowledge about the motivation of donors is critical to successful educational fundraising. Targets might have had different reasons for getting involved and, therefore, for giving. Talking with representatives of the target groups helps to ensure that the right group of donors has, in fact, been targeted. These conversations also help to determine what the exchange process should entail: the message and offer that will produce the best gifts.

No differences may be found among target groups in terms of the educational fundraising appeal. If that is the situation, then the broader cluster or subsegment should be targeted. However, the decision should be based on something more reliable than a hunch or the dictates of a skimpy budget. Experience has shown that it is best to determine the targets who will provide the greatest yields and then pursue them vigorously.

Organizations also form a segment. They can help in the fundraising effort and can also be solicited for funds. There are numerous organizations on campus, including fraternities, sororities, departmental clubs, student government, residence hall associations, and even parents associations.

Corporations that might be targeted in educational fundraising efforts include those that employ graduates or who have a vendor relationship with the institution.

Numerous national and local foundations as well as federal and state agencies fund requests from colleges and universities. Higher education institutions generally have offices that work with foundations and agencies. These offices have detailed information available on foundations and government agencies that should prove helpful. Responding to donor needs is easiest in the case of agencies because they tend to produce requests for proposals, which make their needs known.

In summary, segmenting and targeting of those most likely to give is a critical activity, saving valuable resources of time and money and providing the greatest yield for the effort. Targeting also allows fundraisers to tailor the offer to meet specific donor needs. Very often a carefully targeted appeal will overshadow requests from less sophisticated competition.

Positioning. Almost every day, prospective donors are bombarded by numerous requests for support from countless organizations for many important causes. Positioning strategies help make the institution's request stand out as the most compelling and deserving. In other words, positioning helps the institution's educational fundraising request stand out in the minds of prospective donors by distinguishing it from all of the other requests for funds (Ries and Trout, 1986, pp. 2–3). Therefore, in developing positioning strategies, one obviously has to know not only prospective donors but also competitors.

An example of a very effective positioning strategy is the United Negro College Fund campaign "A Mind Is a Terrible Thing to Waste." Eastern Michigan University uses the slogan "Make a Positive Difference in the Life of an Individual Student." Through this approach, Eastern Michigan has positioned student affairs, creating a very special relationship between the donor and the university, as well as between the donor and student beneficiaries.

Product. Product strategy components are best conceptualized as the offers that are made to prospective donors. The offer should include what the benefits will be to the donor, to the institution, and to those who will ultimately be touched by the gift.

Benefits to a donor might range from personal satisfaction about helping to a building named in the donor's honor. Benefits to the institution might include funds to purchase special equipment, construct a new building, or create an endowment (the gift that keeps on giving, if well managed).

Price. How much money will donors be asked to contribute? How large should a gift be to merit special recognition? Should special donor recognition levels be incorporated? Can the gift be paid over several years? These are only a few examples of strategy decisions that need to be made. The worst educational fundraising pricing strategy is to ask the donor to determine the amount. At a minimum, pricing strategies should include analysis and rating of each donor's ability to give as a basis for establishing an amount that can realistically be solicited. Designation of arbitrary levels for recognition, coupled with the hope that prospective donors will give at the highest level, is not recommended as the most successful strategy. As with all fundraising strategies, research on the market is crucial. In setting giving levels and in soliciting individuals, organizations, foundations, agencies, or corporations, one must know what amount to ask for and what will be given in return (a good feeling, a plaque, naming of a scholarship), and one must establish the expectations, if the effort is to be successful.

Place. Place strategies focus on how individuals become donors, what offices they have worked with and through, and where these offices are located. There are many important policies, procedures, and practices that professional institutional advancement officers have designed over the years for contacting donors and especially for processing their gifts. There are also numerous legal aspects associated with several types of giving. The director of institutional advancement at the university must play a critical role in this strategy area by helping to design approaches that provide the necessary flexibility to accomplish goals but also are consonant with the fundraising approaches of the university as a whole.

Promotions. Promotion strategies are the communication techniques used to inform, persuade, and influence prospective donors to contribute to the educational fundraising cause. Promotion strategies, more often than not, are budget-driven, since there are limited dollars available. Another important consideration in the development of promotion strategies is the tone of communication. In developing communication strategies, the best approach is to put oneself in the place of the prospective donor and ask, "What's in this for me?" When this question is answered, the message and appeal that will work best in reaching prospective donors will be much easier to determine.

In most successful professional educational fundraising activities, a case statement is developed. Usually attractively designed and printed, the statement makes the case for giving and is the key publication in the promotional effort. It is at the core of the persuasive materials provided to donors and is also extremely helpful in training educational fundraising volunteers.

Ideally, a case statement should be written for each target group. However, because of the cost and time involved, this is not always practical. Therefore, the case statement should be written with general appeal to all prospective donors and should be targeted through the use of collateral materials.

Promotions also involve special events and other public relations activities. It is important to recognize the cost of time and dollars for each of the efforts and to determine, as definitively as possible, whether they will significantly aid in achieving overall objectives. An alternate, less costly, and less time-consuming strategy might be just as effective as events that are held just because people enjoy them.

Therefore, in developing promotional strategies, one should consider who is to be reached and what the objective is in doing so. What communication channels will be used? What will the message be? How will it be delivered? At this point, the cost and benefits of each approach should be carefully determined and the promotional strategies refined in terms of human and fiscal resources available to execute them.

Marketing is both an art and a science. It requires one to make numerous decisions and judgments on the basis of limited data, in spite of the availability of limited human and fiscal resources. The point still remains, however, that execution of a plan without the requisite resources to ensure its success is a fatal approach. Not only will this approach result in failure, but it will also create serious difficulty when starting up future activities. In developing strategies for each of the areas explored above, it is helpful to follow a parallel approach. The strategy format outline in the Appendix of this chapter provides useful guidelines for stating each marketing strategy as well as for translating it into specific action steps that will be taken to achieve the desired educational fundraising objectives.

Resources. A common and serious promotional trap that must be avoided is to proceed with only limited dollars available. Many great ideas have failed not because they were flawed but because they were not properly funded. The cliché that one has to spend money to make money is just as true in educational fundraising as it is in business.

Once the plan has been developed, it is necessary to determine the human and fiscal resources required for its implementation, as well as to determine available resources. If there is a gap between the two, it must be reconciled before proceeding. The purpose of planning is to reduce risk and achieve the highest degree of success possible. If resources that are critical to success are unavailable, then it is crucial to determine whether the educational fundraising effort can be implemented. If it cannot, and necessary additional resources are unavailable, do not proceed.

Operations. Time lines and assignments are needed for any managed project. These are integral parts of the strategic marketing process, what needs to be done, when, and by whom should be determined as part of the strategic marketing educational fundraising plan.

Evaluation and Renewal. Evaluation should be an ongoing process in which the educational fundraising effort is fine-tuned as it proceeds. The campus institutional advancement office should be able to assist in this evaluation process. It is important to assess the overall campaign: Was the goal achieved? Who were the major donors and how much did they give? How much did it cost to raise funds?

It is also important to research various components of the campaign. Was one of the mailings more effective than another? Did personal notes to donors written on the campaign literature outperform packets without personal notes? There are many assessment models and approaches that are easy to use and that can help maximize the educational fundraising effort.

The evaluation phase provides the platform for campaign renewal. Results should be discussed with the division of student affairs participants as well as the institutional advancement staff. Evaluation provides the opportunity for understanding the need to modify educational fundraising initiatives and to build continuing support, not only for making the appropriate changes but for creating energy for the following year's efforts.

Appendixes. The strategic marketing educational fundraising plan should be brief so that it is read and used. There will be a considerable amount of material that is related to but not essential to include in the marketing plan. It should be referenced in an appendix, not included in the plan. Materials identified in the appendix should be available from the office most closely related to the planning process.

Conclusion

Marketing is a very complex, rich discipline. A brief chapter can only scratch the surface of its enormous potential for helping student affairs professionals achieve success. Strategic marketing planning is an approach that can make a critical difference in our effectiveness not only in fundraising but also in all other areas within our purview.

Appendix: Strategy Format Outline

Title: Insert the strategy name.

Description: Provide a brief summary of the strategy.

Analysis: Describe the current situation and the benefits to be derived from implementing this strategy.

Principal Indicators: Does this strategy have the greatest impact on identification and qualification of prospective donors, cultivation, solicitations and gifts, or fulfillment and renewal?

Marketing Mix: Does this strategy have the greatest impact on segmentation and targets, positioning, product, price, place (distribution), or promotion?

Action Plans: List steps that will be taken to implement strategy and indicate whether they are urgent (implementation this year), short (implementation during next year), intermediate (implementation during the next two years), or long (implementation during the next three years).

Budget: Will this strategy be funded by general fund, institutional advancement, reallocation, or other?

Type: Does this strategy lead directly to immediate impact on results (action), build a stronger base for further action and results (institutional advancement), or supply information needed for longer term strategic success (analysis)?

References

"AMA Board Approves New Marketing Definition." *Marketing News,* Mar. 1, 1985, p. 1.

Kotler, P., and Andreasen, A. R. *Strategic Marketing for Nonprofit Organizations.* (4th ed.) Englewood Cliffs, N.J.: Prentice Hall, 1991.

Ries, A., and Trout, J. *Positioning: The Battle for Your Mind.* New York: Warner Books, 1986.

LAURENCE N. SMITH is vice president for university marketing and student affairs at Eastern Michigan University, Ypsilanti.

This chapter explores the degree to which student affairs and institutional advancement offices cooperate in raising external funds for student extracurricular activities, and which activities receive the greatest support.

The Relationship Between Student Affairs and Institutional Advancement Offices in Educational Fundraising

Elaine C. Fygetakis, Jon C. Dalton

In recent years, student affairs leaders have increasingly turned to external educational fundraising as a strategy for coping with declining resources and underfunding of student services and extracurricular activities. This strategy has led to greater contact with institutional advancement offices and has, as a result, generated many issues regarding how the two offices communicate, collaborate, and compete on educational fundraising activities. Past research investigating the educational fundraising efforts of student affairs offices has failed to consider the role of institutional advancement offices in such endeavors. While both offices may be raising external funds for student extracurricular activities on their campuses, little information about their activities can be found in either the student affairs or the institutional advancement literature.

In 1991, we conducted a national survey to determine the amount of effort expended on educational fundraising by student affairs and institutional advancement offices for student extracurricular activities. Utilizing cooperation theory as a framework, we explored the degree to which both offices raised external funds and worked together in soliciting contributions for selected extracurricular activities.

Theoretical Framework

Since the relationship between the offices of student affairs and institutional development is critical for the success of student affairs educational fundraising activities, it is important to understand the nature of the alliance between these two organizational units. To examine this connection, the present study applied Deutsch's (1949a, 1949b, 1973, 1980) theory of cooperation and competition as the theoretical framework. According to this theory, the social interaction and productivity of organizations can be understood by investigating how groups perceive their own goals to be related (or unrelated) to those of other groups (Deutsch and Krauss, 1962). In this study, the two groups were institutional advancement offices and student affairs offices. Their mutual goals were to raise external funds for student extracurricular activities.

Deutsch's (1949a, 1949b, 1973, 1980) theory holds that mutually shared goals between groups may be cooperatively (positively), competitively (negatively), or individualistically (independently) linked. In cooperation, groups regard their goal attainments as positively related and work together toward the same outcome. Groups in competition see their goals as negatively linked, and each believes that the other's efforts are interfering with its own goal achievement. Competition is, then, the act of trying to accomplish what another is trying to gain at the same time. When groups are independently linked, they perceive each other's goals as unrelated. In this situation, goal movement may not encourage or discourage the goals of the other group. Overall, the theory holds that cooperatively linked goals are more likely to facilitate greater social interaction and productivity (Tjosvold, 1984, 1986; Tjosvold, Andrews, and Jones, 1983; Johnson and others, 1981).

Some administrators have suggested that student affairs officers need to assess the political climate on their campus in order to ascertain if there will be resistance to their educational fundraising efforts from the institutional advancement office, foundation, or other educational fundraising entities (Kimmel, 1986; Kintigh, 1986). The implication is that student affairs offices may be perceived as competing for scarce resources. A similar implication is that institutional advancement offices may not be initially committed to raise external funds for programs administered by student affairs offices. Deutsch's theory was used to determine if both the student affairs and the institutional advancement offices in the survey sample perceived educational fundraising for student extracurricular activities as mutual goals and, if so, to ascertain which types of relationships (cooperative, competitive, or independent) existed between the two groups when raising external funds for particular activities.

Methodology

An educational fundraising survey was developed based on Deutsch's theory of cooperation and competition and on surveys described in the educational fundraising literature. Two different versions of the survey were distributed, one specifically for institutional advancement offices and the other for student affairs offices. Three other items were included on the student affairs survey for purposes of gathering additional demographic and budget information. Otherwise, the two versions differed only by wording that reflected questions for institutional advancement officers and questions for student affairs personnel.

A cover letter and survey were mailed to chief student affairs officers and chief institutional advancement officers at 159 universities. The sample consisted of large, state-supported institutions with enrollments of ten thousand or more students. Larger institutions were selected as the population to be studied since they were likely to have enough resources to conduct educational fundraising efforts specifically for student extracurricular activities. After completing three separate mailings, a total of 212 usable surveys (67 percent) were received out of a possible 318 surveys. Of the 212 surveys, 100 were returned by institutional advancement offices and 112 by student affairs offices.

Demographic Information

Several items on the survey asked for basic demographic information from both offices. For instance, one survey item asked each respondent to indicate if he or she was the senior administrator in the office. Nearly 52 percent of the student affairs administrators responding to the survey indicated that they were the chief student affairs officers at their institutions. Similarly, 52 percent of the responses to the institutional advancement survey came from chief institutional advancement officers.

Student affairs respondents were asked to indicate if their offices employed their own institutional advancement officers. Fourteen (12.5 percent) of the 112 respondents reported that their offices employed their own institutional advancement officers, while 96 (85.7 percent) indicated that they did not employ their own officers.

Another item on both surveys asked respondents to indicate if an institutional advancement officer was assigned to the student affairs office. Here again, the overwhelming majority (85.6 percent) responded that there was not an institutional advancement officer assigned to perform such duties. Seven institutional advancement offices (7 percent) and 13 student affairs offices (11.6 percent) had an institutional advancement officer assigned to the student affairs office.

Types of Extracurricular Activities
Receiving External Funds

Sixteen extracurricular activities, and one "other" category, were listed on both surveys. Respondents were asked to check all of the programs for which their offices coordinated and conducted educational fundraising activities.

Each of the sixteen activities received multiple responses from both offices and could therefore be conceptualized as mutual goals in educational fundraising. Student affairs offices usually checked the categories far more frequently than their institutional advancement counterparts. Table 5.1 shows the number of responses by both offices, as well as the total number of responses for each activity.

The extracurricular activity of women and minority student programs received the most combined responses. Out of 105 total responses, 70 came from student affairs offices and 35 came from institutional advancement offices. This activity was also the highest-ranked activity by institutional advancement offices. It was the third-ranked activity by student affairs offices. Future educational fundraising studies should consider separating programs for women students and minority students into two distinct categories to help ascertain the extent to which each is being funded.

Ranked second in combined responses was the activity of career planning and development. There were 97 total responses to this category, with 72 coming from student affairs offices and 25 from institutional advancement offices. While student affairs offices had nearly three times the number of the institutional advancement responses, this category was still the third-ranked activity by institutional advancement offices. It was the second-ranked among student affairs offices.

Table 5.1. Frequency Distribution of Educational Fundraising Responses of Institutional Advancement and Student Affairs Offices by Student Extracurricular Activity

Extracurricular Activity	Institutional Advancement (N = 100)	Student Affairs (N = 112)	Total (N = 212)
Alcohol and substance abuse	19	76	95
Career planning and development	25	72	97
Community service and volunteerism	19	58	77
Creative or performing arts	30	51	81
Disabled student issues	22	62	84
Health care, wellness, and personal counseling	12	57	69
Homecoming	20	58	78
Parents weekend	19	56	75
Rape education and campus safety	9	51	60
Recreation programs or equipment	21	58	79
Residence hall construction or renovation	14	49	63
Student recreation center construction or renovation	20	52	72
Student union construction or renovation	19	59	78
Training student leaders	13	59	72
Tutorial and learning centers	13	46	59
Women and minority student programs	35	70	105
Other	17	41	58

Four times as many student affairs offices (76) than institutional advancement offices (19) responded to the third-ranked activity of alcohol and substance abuse programs. This activity was the top-ranked activity for student affairs offices, but it was eighth overall (tied with three other categories) for institutional advancement offices.

Disabled student issues finished fourth overall in combined responses (84). About three times as many student affairs offices (62) than institutional advancement offices (22) responded to this activity. The activity also rated fourth in responses by both the institutional advancement and the student affairs offices.

The fifth-ranked activity in combined responses was creative or performing arts programs. Out of 81 total responses, 30 were from institutional advancement offices and 51 were from student affairs offices. This activity was rated the second highest by institutional advancement offices but was only the thirteenth-rated activity of student affairs offices.

The extracurricular program that received the fewest combined responses was tutorial and learning centers. Nevertheless, 46 student affairs offices and 13 institutional advancement offices indicated that they had raised external funds for such programs. The 46 responses given by student affairs offices were the lowest number of total responses given to any activity by this group of offices. On the other hand, only 9 institutional advancement offices indicated that they had raised external funds for rape education and campus safety programs. While this was the lowest-ranked activity for institutional advancement offices, 51 student affairs offices reported that they had actively raised funds for such programs.

There were three items on the survey that specifically asked about educational fundraising for building construction or renovation projects for residence halls, student unions, and student recreation centers. There were 213 combined responses for construction- and renovation-related activities. These responses give a different view of educational fundraising priorities by surpassing the highest-ranked activity, women and minority student programs (105 combined responses). Of the 213 responses to construction and renovation activities, 53 came from institutional advancement offices and 160 came from student affairs offices. A similar pattern was detectable when total responses for construction or renovation of student recreation centers (72) were combined with those for recreation programs or equipment (79). The 151 total responses for recreation-related activities is also larger than the 105 total responses for the top-ranked activity of women and minority student programs.

An "other" category was included on the list of student extracurricular activities so that offices could indicate educational fundraising activities not listed among the original sixteen categories. This category received 17 responses from institutional advancement offices and 41 responses from student affairs offices. The most frequent category of response pertained to fundraising for scholarships, with responses from 10 student affairs offices and 3 institutional advancement offices. Future researchers may want to investigate educational fundraising by student affairs offices for scholarships, even though it is not an extracurricular program per se.

Other educational fundraising endeavors listed by the two groups of offices included programs such as intercollegiate athletics, cheerleading, early childhood center, senior class gifts, emergency loans or grants, outreach programs, and libraries.

Based on these survey responses, it is clear that both student affairs and institutional advancement offices were actively engaged in raising external funds for a wide variety of student extracurricular activities. This finding, in and of itself, is important in that educational fundraising has been most often associated with securing of external funds for academic programs. Student affairs practitioners interested in starting a program or expanding existing programs with external funding sources should take some comfort in the fact that their colleagues have had success at securing funds for nonacademic programs. Overall, these findings suggest that there may be a campus climate receptive to educational fundraising for student extracurricular activities as well as for academic programs. In the next section, we explore whether or not the educational fundraising efforts for extracurricular programs were perceived in the same way by institutional advancement officers and student affairs personnel in our sample.

Relationship Between Offices in Raising Funds

Offices conducting educational fundraising for specific extracurricular activities were asked to comment on the nature of their relationships with the offices in the other group in these efforts. Both surveys included three possible answers that coincided with Deutsch's theory of cooperation and competition. For each activity that had received external funding, the respondent was asked to determine if the other office "helps," "hinders," or has "no effect" on his or her own office's educational fundraising efforts. Chi-square tests of significance were used to learn if grouping by office affected responses for each of the sixteen extracurricular activities listed on the survey.

In most cases, both groups of offices responded that the other office either had helped or had no effect on educational fundraising for extracurricular activities. There were only three instances of a "hinders" response for a specific extracurricular activity. One student affairs office indicated that the institutional advancement office had hindered educational fundraising efforts in the area of career planning and development. Two different institutional advancement offices gave the "hinders" response to student affairs offices, one for the activity of homecoming and the other for women and minority student programs. Overall, most responses suggested that there was little strife between offices when raising external funds for student extracurricular activities.

For twelve activities, significant differences were found between the observed and expected responses of institutional advancement offices and student affairs offices. Readers are cautioned to consider that for six of these twelve activities—residence hall construction or renovation; health care, wellness, and personal counseling; homecoming; rape education and campus safety; tutorial and learning centers; and women and minority student programs—there may not have been a large enough sample size to support the findings of significance with confidence.

For the other six activities with significant differences—alcohol and substance abuse programs ($p < .001$), student union construction or renovation ($p < .001$), student recreation center construction or renovation ($p < .002$), community service and volunteerism ($p < .001$), recreation programs or equipment ($p < .001$), and training student leaders ($p < .005$)—institutional advancement offices more frequently responded that their student affairs offices helped them to raise funds for these extracurricular activities. However, student affairs offices more frequently responded that the institutional advancement offices had no effect on raising external funds. In terms of Deutsch's theory, these findings suggest that institutional advancement offices were more frequently inclined to view their mutual educational fundraising efforts for these activities as positively cooperatively linked with those of student affairs offices. On the other hand, student affairs offices were more frequently viewing their educational fundraising efforts as independent from those of the institutional advancement offices.

Four activities (career planning and development, creative or performing arts, disabled student issues, and parents weekend) did not yield significant differences. In other words, both groups of offices were inclined to view the actions of the other group in the same way. With the exception of parents weekend, the three other activities ranked in the top-five of total educational fundraising responses. This means that student affairs and institutional advancement offices usually perceived the actions of the other group in the same way, for three of five activities receiving the greatest numbers of educational fundraising responses. This was not the case for another top-ranked activity, alcohol and substance abuse programs. As previously described, the two groups of offices perceived the educational fundraising actions of the other in different ways for this activity. Not enough data were available to determine the relationship between the offices for the top-ranked activity, women and minority student programs.

Total Dollars Raised for Student Extracurricular Activities

Respondents from both groups of offices were asked to estimate the total dollars raised from external sources during a period of three fiscal years

(July 1, 1988, through June 30, 1991). Fifty-four student affairs offices and 30 institutional advancement offices responded with actual dollar amounts. Table 5.2 shows the ranges of dollars raised by all 84 offices responding to the item. Many respondents from both offices indicated that they were unable to provide actual dollar amounts because the calculation was too time-consuming or the amount was too difficult to determine. Some of these same offices were able to provide other funding information for specific activities, although these amounts could not be included as "total dollars."

For the 30 institutional advancement offices and 54 student affairs offices responding, the median amount of total dollars raised by both groups of offices was $100,000. The lowest amount indicated was $300 (by a student affairs office), while the maximum amount reported was approximately $5.6 million (by an institutional advancement office). Since there was a very broad range in total dollars raised—and therefore a "skewed distribution"—the

Table 5.2. Frequency Distribution of Total External Dollars
Raised by Institutional Advancement and Student Affairs
Offices for Student Extracurricular Programs

External Dollars Raised	Frequency	Cumulative Frequency	Cumulative Percentage
1–10,000	19	19	22.6
10,001–20,000	2	21	25.0
20,001–30,000	2	23	27.4
30,001–40,000	5	28	33.3
40,001–50,000	3	31	36.9
50,001–60,000	5	36	42.9
60,001–70,000	1	37	44.0
70,001–80,000	3	40	47.6
80,001–90,000	1	41	48.8
90,001–100,000	2	43	51.2
100,001–200,000[a]	12	55	65.5
200,001–300,000	5	60	71.4
300,001–400,000	2	62	73.8
400,001–500,000	4	66	78.6
500,001–600,000	2	68	81.0
600,001–700,000	0	68	81.0
700,001–800,000	4	72	85.7
800,001–900,000	1	73	86.9
900,001–1,000,000	2	75	89.3
1,000,001–2,000,000	2	77	91.7
2,000,001–3,000,000	3	80	95.2
3,000,001–4,000,000	2	82	97.6
4,000,001–5,000,000	1	83	98.8
5,000,001+	1	84	100

Note: Total dollars reflect amounts raised from July 1, 1988, through June 30, 1991; median = $100,000, minimum = $300, maximum = $5,603,000, M = $510,192.65, SD = $1,035,501.33.

[a] Intervals change at this point.

median is provided for a more accurate picture of actual dollars raised from external sources.

Some offices were more vigorous than others in raising external funds. While 19 offices raised no more than $10,000, 9 offices raised more than $1 million. The maximum amount raised by a student affairs office was slightly over $4.2 million, while the maximum raised by an institutional advancement office was slightly over $5.6 million. Similarly, the minimum amounts reported were $300 by a student affairs office and $500 by an institutional advancement office. The median for student affairs offices was $116,000, and the median for institutional advancement offices was $87,500.

Conclusion

In our survey, we found that many institutional advancement and student affairs offices at large, public institutions were engaged in raising external funds for student extracurricular activities. These offices therefore had a mutual goal to raise external funds for student extracurricular activities.

As might be expected, student affairs offices were more frequently engaged in such endeavors than were institutional advancement offices. This finding may suggest that, in general, student affairs offices engage in educational fundraising activities independently of institutional advancement offices. Indeed, this was often the complaint of institutional advancement offices in our sample. On the other hand, student affairs staff may be engaged in certain educational fundraising activities because they perceive that they will receive no help from their institutional advancement offices. It is clearly beneficial for both offices to have mutual agreements about the goals and procedures of educational fundraising for all student extracurricular activities.

How each group perceived the other's efforts to raise external funds varied, depending on the extracurricular activity. Educational fundraising endeavors for certain extracurricular activities were typically perceived as cooperatively or independently linked, with little suggestion of competition between the offices. One of the most gratifying findings of this study is that, on the whole, student affairs and institutional advancement offices viewed their relationships in educational fundraising activities as positive and cooperative. This is an important finding because student affairs organizations will likely increase their educational fundraising activities in the future.

This study also identified some types of extracurricular activities for which external funds are frequently sought and for which there is considerable cooperation between student affairs and institutional advancement offices. These activities may serve as worthy starting points for student affairs organizations initiating educational fundraising activities.

We suggest that the student affairs office attempt to coordinate a comprehensive educational fundraising strategy for each of its departments.

One obvious way to begin is to have each administrative area develop a "wish list" of program priorities. Administrative staff and students could help identify specific needs. (Faculty feedback could also be solicited, if appropriate). Deans or directors of these areas could also contact their own peers (for example, career counseling directors contacting directors at other institutions) regarding their expertise in securing grants or other funding sources for specific projects. Professional organizations may be able to provide useful information as well.

After identifying projects of priority, consultation with other administrative heads should be pursued to discuss courses of action. Indeed, some units may choose to work together on a specific project (for example, residence hall life with the counseling center on acquaintance rape). A centralized "student affairs educational fundraising committee" may be formed, for ongoing consultation, implementation, and evaluation of educational fundraising efforts. Alumni affairs, sponsored research, and institutional advancement offices could also be consulted to determine potential funding sources and alternative courses of action.

It is important for student affairs leaders to establish formal educational fundraising goals with their institutional advancement offices so that there is mutual understanding and support for each other's activities. The present research shows that both offices are actively engaged in soliciting funds for student extracurricular activities.

Finally, this study indicates that very few student affairs organizations have their own institutional advancement officers. No doubt this reflects the newness of external educational fundraising as an organizational priority for student affairs as well as a practical resource issue. If, however, external educational fundraising is to become an important strategy of resource development for student affairs, the need for a student affairs development officer may be a future staffing priority.

References

Deutsch, M. "An Experimental Study of the Effects of Co-Operation and Competition upon Group Process." *Human Relations,* 1949a, 2, 199–231.

Deutsch, M. "A Theory of Co-Operation and Competition." *Human Relations,* 1949b, 2, 129–152.

Deutsch, M. *The Resolution of Conflict.* New Haven, Conn.: Yale University Press, 1973.

Deutsch, M. "Fifty Years of Conflict." In L. Festinger (ed.), *Retrospections on Social Psychology.* New York: Oxford University Press, 1980.

Deutsch, M., and Krauss, R. M. "Studies in Interpersonal Bargaining." *Journal of Conflict Resolution,* 1962, 6, 52–76.

Johnson, D. W., and others. "Effects of Cooperative, Competitive, and Individualistic Goal Structures on Achievement: A Meta-Analysis." *Psychological Bulletin,* 1981, 89, 47–62.

Kimmel, R. B. "Fund Raising in Student Affairs: Thrust for the Future?" *College Student Affairs Journal,* 1986, 6 (4), 5–10.

Kintigh, C. "Building a Successful Fund Raising Program." *Campus Activities Programming,* 1986, 19, 46–49.

Tjosvold, D. "Cooperation Theory and Organizations." *Human Relations,* 1984, *37,* 743–767.
Tjosvold, D. "The Dynamics of Interdependence in Organizations." *Human Relations,* 1986, *39,* 517–540.
Tjosvold, D., Andrews, R., and Jones, H. "Cooperative and Competitive Relationships Between Leaders and Subordinates." *Human Relations,* 1983, *36,* 1111–1124.

ELAINE C. FYGETAKIS recently received a Ph.D. in higher education administration from the Department of Educational Leadership, Florida State University, Tallahassee.

JON C. DALTON is vice president for student affairs and associate professor in the Department of Educational Leadership, Florida State University.

Funds awarded for grant and contract activities provide additional resources and enhancements for student affairs units. This chapter presents an overview of student affairs involvement in grant and contract activity.

Involvement of Student Affairs Administrators in Grant-Writing Activities

Joe L. Davis, Sharon K. Davis

Solicitation of funds through grant and contract proposals for extramural support (funds from noncollege or university sources) is an expected and normal activity in institutions of higher education. Grant and contract activity is an anticipated and rewarded endeavor for faculty; however, grant writing for student affairs staff receives little attention on most college campuses. There is a dearth of information concerning grant and contract activity in student affairs. The professional literature describes several aspects of grant writing in institutions of higher education (for example, Davis, 1988; Hickey and King, 1988; Holleman, 1989; Johnston, 1989). These publications report on a variety of topics: preparing proposals, increasing the number of proposals developed, and the volume and type of extramural funding received. But not one describes grant and contract activity as it relates to student affairs. The student affairs area is not listed, cited, or mentioned in the publications.

In this chapter, we describe the results of a national survey of chief student affairs officers (CSAOs) that focused on grant and contract activity. The level of encouragement, support, and success of student affairs units in developing proposals and securing extramural funds, institutional assistance, and sources of funding are featured topics. In addition, we detail how student affairs staff can write successful proposals.

The population for the survey consisted of the 951 CSAOs identified as members of the National Association of Student Personnel Administrators in spring 1991. An instrument to measure grant and contract activity in student affairs was designed specifically for this project. A pilot test of the survey instrument was conducted during summer 1991. The mail survey conducted during fall 1991 resulted in a 51 percent return rate. The 485 completed survey instruments provided the data for the analysis. Nine completed instruments returned from institutions outside the United States were not included.

Previous work by Davis (1988) identified four categories of assessment for grant and contract activity at universities: expectations, level of activity, incentives, and support. Davis reported the grant activity in four-year institutions with enrollments under seventy-five hundred students and fewer than four hundred faculty. The four categories identified for the present study have a high degree of face validity and are applicable to large as well as small institutions.

Expectations

The expectation for student affairs staff to develop proposals and receive grant awards was significant. An overwhelming majority of the CSAOs (81 percent) indicated that it was important for their staffs to write proposals for extramural funding. These administrators (80 percent) saw a need to increase the numbers of proposals developed by their staffs.

Institutions of higher education also place expectations on individuals for grant-writing activities. The CSAOs reported that 65 percent of their institutions expected faculty to develop proposals for extramural funding; this figure compared to 41 percent of the institutions expecting student affairs staff to develop proposals for extramural funding. The expectations for academic administrators compared to student affairs administrators were 56 percent and 41 percent, respectively.

A majority (89 percent) of the CSAOs reported that they encouraged student affairs staff to develop proposals for extramural funding. This stance was supported by the finding that during the prior three academic years (1988–1991) the percentage of students affairs units reporting *zero* proposal submissions declined from 28 percent to 15 percent. More student affairs units were submitting proposals seeking extramural funds.

Level of Activity

CSAOs reported that grant and contract activity greatly increased during the years 1988–1991. This increase in the level of activity was noted in the amounts of major awards received by institutions, the variety of categories funded, and the number of institutions reporting success in receiving funded projects.

During this same period, the percentage of institutions that developed proposals seeking $100,000 to $250,000 increased from 14 percent to 19 percent, and the percentage of institutions developing proposals for more than $250,000 increased from 13 percent to 19 percent. Thus, student affairs units were expanding their efforts to garner extramural funds to assist in accomplishing their mission.

The level of activity for funded projects extended over a broad range. "College student support services" was reported as the purpose for developing a proposal for extramural funding by 70 percent of the CSAOs. This was more than double the 32 percent who reported "recruit underrepresented groups" as the purpose of seeking funds. The next level of activity was "public services" with 29 percent of the CSAOs seeking extramural funding, followed by 27 percent of the CSAOs seeking funds for "precollege student support."

The real measure of success in extramural funding can be seen in the change in the number and amount of awards received by student affairs units over an extended time. The percentage of institutions reporting zero extramural proposals funded declined from 36 percent in 1988–1989 to 23 percent in 1990–1991. This finding reveals definite progress in securing extramural funding by student affairs units. During this same period, the percentage of institutions awarded between $100,000 to $250,000 increased from 12 percent to 17 percent. The percentage receiving more than $250,000 increased from 10 percent to 15 percent. These figures indicate that student affairs units were increasingly successful in securing extramural funds for their projects.

Incentives

Many types of incentives can be used to motivate individuals to submit proposals for extramural funding. These incentives include activities benefiting the individual or activities benefiting the student affairs unit. Incentives benefiting the individual include promotion and tenure, part of employee evaluation, and increase in salary or personal recognition. Incentives benefiting the student affairs unit include increased resources and special recognition.

Incentives for the Individual. In our survey, 75 percent of the CSAOs reported that "recognition (pat-on-back)" was the incentive used most often to motivate staff to develop proposals. The second most often used incentive was "part of employee evaluation," a method reported by 47 percent of the CSAOs. "Retain employment, if on extramural funds" was reported by 20 percent of the CSAOs. This method was closely followed by 14 percent reporting "salary increase" for the proposal writer. Eleven percent indicated that some "other form" of incentive was available, and 10 percent reported "no incentives" were used to motivate their student affairs staffs to develop proposals for extramural funding.

Incentives for the Unit. Institutions often use some portion of the indirect funds generated by extramural awards as an incentive or as a method of increasing the number of proposals developed by campus entities. In our survey, 16 percent of the CSAOs reported using "proposal author's unit retains salary savings generated" as an incentive for developing proposals for funding. The CSAOs reported that 27 percent of their institutions used "allocated to the unit generating the indirect funds" as the method to disperse the generated indirect funds. This was followed by 26 percent of the CSAOs reporting that indirect funds were "divided among various institutional units on a formula basis." Twenty-four percent of the CSAOs reported that "100 percent to general revenue" was the method used to disperse generated indirect funds. A sizable number (18 percent) of the CSAOs indicated that they did not know how indirect funds were handled by their institutions.

The disbursement of actual funds awarded by extramural agencies is normally governed by explicitly detailed formulas in the proposal budgets. Most funding agencies expect indirect cost to be a part of the project cost. Certainly, most federal and state agencies have an indirect cost rate stated in the request for proposal (RFP). Most institutions have one or more indirect cost rates negotiated with federal agencies. Proposal writers should be familiar with these rates and include indirect cost as part of the project budget. The method of disbursing indirect funds by the institution is an internal decision. The CSAO, as a major corporate officer of the institution, should be involved in developing the policy governing disbursal of recovered indirect funds generated by grant and contract activity.

In our survey, the responding CSAOs indicated that 74 percent of the student affairs units do not receive a portion of the recovered indirect funds, 14 percent indicated that student affairs units do receive a portion; and 9 percent did not know whether their units received any recovered indirect funds. Seventy-five percent of the CSAOs reported that indirect funds generated by awards to student affairs were treated the same as indirect funds generated by other units, 8 percent indicated that recovered indirect funds were handled differently, and 9 percent responded that they did not know how such funds were handled.

Support

The task of writing proposals for extramural funding is difficult and time-consuming for all but a few extraordinary people. Most faculty and student affairs staff are not attuned to the fine points of grant writing and thus are in need of training and assistance to be successful grant writers. Institutions of higher education often have an office dedicated to assisting or supporting employees seeking extramural grants and contracts. The CSAOs reported that 78 percent of their institutions provided such an office to assist staff in proposal development, and 20 percent reported that no such office existed to assist individuals. However, 11 percent of the CSAOs reported that their student affairs units had a person or office dedicated to helping staff develop proposals seeking extramural funds.

Training activities for student affairs staff were most often provided by "workshops at professional meetings," as reported by 50 percent of the CSAOs. "Institutionwide grant-writing workshops" was the next most widely available training mechanism, reported by 45 percent of the CSAOs. "Mentoring with experienced grant writers" was reported by 41 percent of the CSAOs. "Grant-writing workshops specifically for student affairs staff" was reported by 7 percent of the CSAOs. Nineteen percent of the CSAOs reported that no training was available for student affairs staff to support proposal development.

Writing Successful Grant Proposals

The writing of successful grant proposals is important not only to student affairs staff but also to the student services unit and to the university. Billions of dollars are awarded each year to those individuals and organizations who prepare successful proposals (Meador, 1985); this fact emphasizes the importance of grant-writing skills.

Getting Started. Development of successful proposals is an ongoing activity. Grant writers must be mindful of the need to prepare proposals that are worthy of funding. Successful grant writers are aware that federal agencies and foundations have specific goals that they are attempting to accomplish; these writers thus develop proposals that will further the aims of the agencies and foundations. This approach is different from that of individuals and institutions who are concerned only with what grant awards will do for their goals.

Grant-writing assistance is available for student affairs staff at most colleges and universities. Larger institutions have established offices that are commonly labeled Office of Sponsored Programs or Grants and Contracts Office. In most offices of sponsored programs, a multitude of services are provided. Student affairs staff will find sources of funding for their projects; application forms for agencies and foundations; assistance in designing projects, developing project budgets, and completing required forms; review of assurance and compliance issues; and individuals who acquire the authorized university signatures. In addition, the office of sponsored programs will duplicate, package, and mail the proposal to the funding agency.

An office of sponsored programs welcomes the opportunity to serve student affairs staff. Student affairs staff can best use these services by setting up an appointment with a grant specialist. The grant specialist then visits briefly with them and suggests that they complete an interest inventory. This interest inventory becomes part of a campus data base, allowing the office to find sources of funding that match the interests of the student affairs staff.

Preparing to Write Successful Proposals. The task of writing successful proposals takes time and effort. The goal is to sell one's ideas and win a contract. As preparation for writing a proposal, there are several steps that can be taken.

Read the RFP. Secure a copy of the RFP and read it a minimum of three times, or as often as needed to understand the goals of the funding agency, the agency requirements, and the agency restrictions.

Develop a Proposal Outline. The RFP outlines the major themes and areas that the agency is interested in funding. A proposal must be organized so that evaluators can easily follow its theme, logic, and activities; evaluators must be able to determine if agency requirements have been met. The proposal outline should follow the guidelines set forth in the RFP.

Develop a Proposal Theme. A proposal theme is the backbone of the project; it expresses in a single statement the purpose of the project. The theme is frequently found in the title or as an acronym. The goals and activities are formulated to address the theme.

Basic Parts of the Proposal. The basic elements of proposals are fairly consistent; there are slight variations. By carefully reading the RFP, the writer determines the exact agency requirements. The proposal includes the following basic parts.

Cover Letter. The cover letter introduces the college or university and student affairs unit and highlights special features of the proposal. It also outlines the basic components and the objectives of the project and briefly states the project benefits.

Title Page. The title page announces the project. The title page format is provided by federal agencies and its use is required. Foundations may not have a title page; in this case, it is advisable to create one. Items generally included on the title page are title of the project, name of the project director, institution submitting the project (name and location of the college or university), organization to which the project is being submitted (name of funding source), cost of the project, duration of the project, and date the project is submitted.

Table of Contents. The table of contents is designed to assist the evaluators in rating the proposal. If the RFP outlines a format, follow it without deviation. This adherence to form is in the best interests of the grant seeker; evaluators frequently use the format in reviewing proposals; there is no need to confuse them.

Abstract. This one-page summary of the project is obligatory and demands thoughtful preparation. The abstract should capture the theme, essence, and tone of the project. It must be clear and it must motivate the evaluator.

Although the abstract is the first part of the project proposal that is read by the evaluators, it is best to write the abstract after the other parts of the proposal have been completed. Many agencies stipulate areas to be addressed in the abstract. If there are no stipulations, the grant writer should identify himself or herself and his or her accomplishments and succinctly state the need for the project, objectives of the project, activities outlined in the project, and benefits of the project. The abstract should also incorporate a statement on how the project meets the funding source's priorities.

Introduction. The introduction is used to establish one's credibility. In this section, one's qualifications, experience, and resources are discussed. The strengths of the institution and student affairs unit also should be detailed. An effective introduction describes the goals, accomplishments, and successes of the unit. Grant writers should use this section to help evaluators become familiar with them and their institutions.

Problem or Need Statement. This section addresses the problems outlined in the RFP. The need statement specifically identifies the problems that the proposed project will solve and establishes distinct connections among this need, the proposed project, and the goals, objectives, and activities of the student affairs unit.

This section documents the problem by using statistical data or information gleaned from national as well as institutional surveys. It outlines how the grant seeker plans to address a local or state problem in a way that could in turn serve as a model for a national program. The following is an example of an introductory paragraph of a need statement:

> The need for drug education programs for young people is paramount. As reported by the U.S. Department of Education (1987), Americans consistently identified drug use as one of the dominant problems facing our nation's schools. Johnston, O'Malley, and Bachman's (1988) analysis of a representative sample of both public and private high schools revealed that no high school is completely drug free. Data from *Drug Use Among American High School Seniors, College Students, and Young Adults, 1975– 1990* (Johnson, O'Malley, and Bachman, 1991) suggest that greater than half of all 1989 seniors reported illicit drug use at some time in their lives. These startling reports illustrate a need for the subsequent implementation of this project.

Objectives. Once the need has been established, the next logical step is to describe the project and what it will do to address the agency needs. The objectives of the project should be listed, and each should specifically describe what will be accomplished as a result of the project. The objectives provide a checklist for evaluating the success of the completed project. The objectives should be concrete and outline results that can be measured, attained, and readily identified when accomplished. Objectives must be realistic. The evaluators are experienced professionals in the field; they do not accept objectives that are unrealistic.

The following are examples of realistic objectives for a project: (1) By the end of the project, 180 facilitators will have completed a training program emphasizing an interdisciplinary approach to educating youth regarding drugs and alcohol. (2) After completing the training, each facilitator will conduct a minimum of five clock hours of workshops on drug and alcohol education. Approximately 15 individuals will attend each workshop. (3) At the completion of the project, at least 2,700 individuals will have completed the training workshops.

Benefits. The benefits of the project are closely related to the objectives. This section is frequently used to describe the benefits at the local or state level and describes how the project could serve as a national model.

Description of the Project. The project description is the focus and central element of the proposal. This section provides a statement of the problem, the need for the project, and the objectives of the project and details how the project objectives will be achieved.

As the work plan is developed, the methods and activities of the project are outlined, and how they will accomplish the objectives is described. A common format used is to state the objectives, outline the methods or activities that will be pursued to meet the objectives, describe when the activities will begin and end, and describe who will conduct the activities.

The project description reflects the planning and analysis of the entire project: the methods, activities, facilities, staff, equipment, supplies, materials, and the time frame. Project descriptions should be specific and precisely outline what steps will be taken to reach the objectives.

The project description must be clear and provide sufficient information to ensure evaluator confidence that the objectives can and will be accomplished. Enough detail must be provided to convince the evaluators that the results will be measurable. The following is an example of an introductory portion of a project description:

The project focuses on eight major components:

1. Formation of an institution wide advisory council
2. Identification of the participants for training
3. Provision of instruction to the identified participants
4. Establishment of a support network among participants .
5. Support and follow-up of participants
6. Evaluation (formative and summative)
7. Dissemination of information at local, state, and national meetings
8. Continuation of project beyond funding period

Time Frame. The time frame provides a chronological map of the project. It provides a reference for everyone participating in the plan. The schedule for each task or activity is outlined, noting both the starting and ending points.

The time frame is frequently presented in a format such as a Gantt chart (Hall, 1988). In this format, specific tasks or subtasks are listed down the left-hand side of the chart; across the top is a time line indicating the duration of the task or the month when each task will be completed. Other commonly used formats are outlines of project schedules and program evaluation review technique charts.

Continuation Funding. Proposal writers need to be alert to the fact and understanding early in the planning of a project that funding agencies have goals that they want to accomplish with limited resources. Each year, funding agencies establish annual budgets and make budget awards within the limits of these established budgets. Agency budgets are developed with the intent of providing funds for innovative projects as well as start-up funds or initial support for new programs. Agency budgets are not designed to provide continuous, long-term support for projects.

As a project is being developed, a proposal writer can plan for one year of funding, or perhaps for as many as three years of funding, from an agency. Agencies will inform the writer of the agency regulations regarding the length of time a project will be funded.

In view of this funding limit, the proposal writer is well advised to develop a project that can be self-sufficient following the initial start-up period. This requires activities that are developed during the grant period and can be continued after the funding obligations of the agency have been met. Examples of such grant activities are developing all materials during the term of the grant, providing for a training manual or training program to train a cadre of individuals during the term of the grant, establishing an advisory board to assume responsibility for acquiring continuous funding, and integrating a community agency or institutional unit into the project that will assume responsibility for continuation of the project.

Evaluation. The evaluation section is important. It provides accountability by outlining how the grant seeker plans to demonstrate the success of the project. This section answers the questions, Did the project accomplish its purpose? Did the project operate as it was designed? What conclusions can be drawn?

This section must also outline how the project will be evaluated. Consideration should be given to record keeping, frequency of evaluation, methods employed to evaluate, and the need for an external evaluator.

Dissemination of Information. Public dissemination of information is vital to a project. It is anticipated that the project will benefit individuals, institutions, states, or the nation. This information should be shared so that others may benefit. Dissemination of project data is important to the funding source and serves as a good public relations tool both for the funding agency and for the grantee institution. Dissemination of information can take many forms, including a published report or a presentation at a local, state, or national professional conference.

Key Project Personnel. An essential component of the project includes the qualifications and experiences of all personnel. The résumés of key staff should be included in an appendix of the proposal.

The project description defines who has responsibility for each task in the project. It is important to indicate that these individuals are highly qualified, capable, and experienced. The credentials of team members are strongly considered by funding officials.

Administrative Procedures (Organizational Chart). The total management of the project, such as monitoring the progress and working toward the achievement of the goals, is important to evaluators and the funding source. The proposal should clearly identify the administrative provisions established to ensure the success and smooth functioning of the project. The higher in the chain of command the project director reports, the better.

Budget. The budget and budget justification should address the economic feasibility of the project. The budget must be realistic and sufficient to accomplish the purposes of the project. In developing a budget, the grant writer must justify all items and relate them to the methods and activities proposed. The budget must be harmonious with the proposed objectives and activities.

Many sponsoring agencies prefer to see, and may require, matching funds from applicants. The availability of matching funds usually has a positive impact on the funding decision. Project directors must work with their student affairs units and their institutions to determine what matching funds are available for the projects.

Although the grant writer may submit a realistic and complete budget to the funding source, it is common to be asked to negotiate the budget at a later date. Be prepared to restrict personnel time and reduce other areas of the budget. This may result in elimination of one or more of the planned objectives or activities.

Appendixes. The RFP may stipulate precisely what materials may be included in the proposal appendixes; these guidelines should be followed. General guidelines suggest that the appendixes provide background information and documentation that support the project. Items frequently included are staff résumés, letters of support and recommendation, additional documentation of materials used in the main body of the proposal, and examples of supplementary or supporting materials.

Bibliography. The source references provided in this section should indicate the thoroughness of one's research and understanding of the technical details. The sources of information used to justify the need for the project and for the project methods and activities are all included.

Tips on Proposal Writing

Key considerations in writing a successful proposal are writing quality, style, and clarity. Technical language should be used in the proposal only as necessary, and professional jargon should be avoided. Each proposal is reviewed by a team of readers. Not everyone on the review team may recognize professional jargon, such as Total Quality Management or TQM.

The writing style should be consistent. The proposal should be consistent in the use of terminology and facts, and in organization (Reif-Lehrer, 1989). For example, for consistency in statements of fact, the writer would note that there are 2,473 students enrolled in Southwest University, not an approximate enrollment of 3,000 students. The precise figure would be used in the objectives, the evaluation, and all other parts of the proposal.

Direct and positive statements indicate to the evaluator that the grant writer has confidence in the project. As an example, it is appropriate to state that "Southwest University is a leader in this geographical region; it has exhibited leadership in bringing together several experts to develop this proposal." The case should be stated succinctly and categorically and supported with evidence, as in the following example: "The project is a collaborative undertaking involving the Student Affairs Division, the College of Education, and the State Alcohol and Drug Abuse Council. Letters of commitment from these organizations are attached. The combined efforts of this select leadership group will enhance and strengthen the network concept."

Use the active rather than the passive voice to strengthen the presentation and to persuade the evaluators that the plan is a good one and that all tasks outlined in the project can be completed. The following is an active voice example: "We shall establish this program by using a network concept. We shall identify individuals at Southwest University from the Division of Student Affairs, the College of Education, and from Student Government. In addition, we shall select individuals from the staff of the State Alcohol and Drug Abuse Council to serve on the Project Advisory Council."

Technical writing aids are beneficial to the grant writer in producing a quality finished product. There are many commercial computer programs available to help the writer check the manuscript for spelling, grammar, and other technical details. In addition, it is helpful to solicit assistance from a colleague to critique and proofread the manuscript prior to its submission to the agency.

Conclusion and Recommendations

Approximately 90 percent of the CSAOs in our survey viewed extramural funding as important. The years 1988–1991 showed a marked increase in the number of student affairs units seeking extramural funds. On the basis of the CSAOs' view of the need to increase the number of proposals developed, it is likely that an even greater number of proposals will be written by student affairs staff in the future. These extramural funds enhance specific student affairs programs and provide opportunities to expand services to students.

The increased number of proposals for competitively based funds points to a need to increase the quality and quantity of proposals developed by student affairs staff. It also points to a greater need for student affairs units to use and cooperate with the institutional office of sponsored programs. The student affairs administrators in our study also identified a lack of training opportunities for student affairs staff in proposal development. Student affairs administrators must take a more active role in the governance issues relating to disbursement of recovered indirect costs, development of rewards systems for individuals and units who develop proposals, and expansion of institutional efforts to secure extramural funds.

References

Davis, S. K. "Research Administration at Predominantly Undergraduate Institutions with a Small Volume of Sponsored Programs." *Research Management Review,* 1988, 2 (2), 41–51.

Hall, M. *Getting Funded: A Complete Guide to Proposal Writing.* (3rd ed.) Portland, Oreg.: Continuing Education, Portland State University, 1988.

Hickey, A. A., and King, K. W. "A Model for Integrating Research Administration and Graduate School Operations at a Regional Comprehensive University." *Research Management Review,* 1988, 2 (1), 31–43.

Holleman, P. "Grants Opportunities for Community College LRC's." *Community and Junior College Libraries,* 1989, 6 (2), 35–42.

Johnston, L. D., O'Malley, P. M., and Bachman, J. G. *Illicit Drug Use, Smoking and Drinking by America's High School Students, College Students and Young Adults, 1975–1987.* Rockville, Md.: National Institute on Drug Abuse, 1988.

Johnston, L. D., O'Malley, P. M., and Bachman, J. G. *Drug Use Among American High School Seniors, College Students, and Young Adults, 1975–1990.* Vol. 1. Washington, D.C.: Government Printing Office, 1991.

Johnston, W. "Tips on Obtaining Grants for the Community College LRC." *Community and Junior College Libraries,* 1989, 6 (2), 43–51.

Meador, R. *Guidelines for Preparing Proposals.* Chelsea, Mich.: Lewis, 1985.

Reif-Lehrer, L. *Writing a Successful Grant Application.* (2nd ed.) Boston: Jones and Barlett, 1989.

U.S. Department of Education. *What Works: Schools Without Drugs.* Publication No. 1987-178-865. Washington, D.C.: Government Printing Office, 1987.

JOE L. DAVIS is chair of the Counseling Department at the University of Nebraska, Omaha.

SHARON K. DAVIS is director of the Office of Sponsored Programs at the University of Nebraska, Lincoln.

Sources of grant funding for cultural diversity programs are presented. The relationship between the level of external funding and institutional priorities at research universities is explored.

The Role of External Funding for Cultural Diversity Programming

Melvin C. Terrell, Donna E. Rudy, Harold E. Cheatham

Development or expansion of programs to improve the recruitment and retention of minority students has been and continues to be an important initiative for student affairs professionals. In a 1988 survey of chief student affairs officers in region 4 of the National Association of Student Personnel Administrators, 89 percent of the respondents indicated that their institutions sponsored cultural diversity programs (Jones, Terrell, and Duggar, 1991). However, success in finding enough additional funds in the institutional budget during this current period of downsizing and cutbacks seems unlikely. External funding may yield an appropriate supplement to institutional funds or an alternative source of financial resources to adequately fund programs designed to assist minority students.

Cultural diversity can be defined in many ways. Levine (1991) presented four definitions: raising the numbers of underrepresented students and faculty, offering compensatory education and support services, encouraging participation in cocurriculum activities, and creating a tolerant campus culture.

This chapter begins with an exploration of the relationship between the role of external funding and the level of institutional commitment to cultural diversity. Then, grant sources such as government agencies and corporations that have targeted funds for cultural diversity programs in higher education are described. Next, we examine elements of successful recruitment and retention programs for minority students that are frequently cited in the literature. Finally, we report the results of a survey research study on the funding sources of cultural diversity programs at U.S. research universities.

New Directions for Student Services, no. 63, Fall 1993 © Jossey-Bass Publishers

Institutional Commitment and the Level of Grant Support

To determine the appropriate level of grant support, it is important to discern if the top leadership views minority student programming as a high priority. If so, they probably have taken the following steps: inclusion of cultural diversity in the institutional mission statement; establishment of hiring goals for a diverse faculty and administration; coordination of training programs for faculty, staff, and students; and maintenance of a system of rewards and punishments for behavior relating to a hospitable campus climate (Stewart, 1991). This kind of support constitutes what Cheatham (1989) termed "institutional signature."

If cultural diversity programming appears to be a high institutional priority, student affairs professionals may employ the strategy of pursuing supplementary grant funds as opposed to funds to support the cost of the entire program. In this way, the leadership can demonstrate their support for the program by making a budgetary commitment in a tight money environment. At the same time, a percentage of the program expenses will be paid by an external source.

If cultural diversity programming does not appear to be a high institutional priority, an appropriate strategy may be to attempt to support the entire program with grant funds. In this way, the top leadership will be less inclined to veto the project, knowing that there is no expectation of institutional funding. Eventually, if the program is successful, cultural diversity programming may become a higher priority to the institution.

Sources of Funding for Cultural Diversity Programming

The most helpful reference for locating grant sources is the *Minority Funding Report,* a monthly summary of federal and corporate financial opportunities for disadvantaged and minority groups. Each issue contains descriptions of grants, relevant federal policies, legislative outlook for bills targeting minorities, and federal commission rules about the process of awarding grants.

The federal government has been active in funding programs for minority students in higher education. Federal grants have supported the Trio programs, which have been providing services to low-income students, particularly minority students, since 1967. More than 40 percent of Trio participants are African American, 35 percent are white, 17 percent are Hispanic, 4 percent are American Indian, and 3 percent are Asian American. More than a quarter of a $197 million increase in the federal budget for higher education was allocated to Trio programs in fiscal year (FY) 1992 ("Trio Programs Prosper . . . ," 1991).

Trio consists of the following programs targeted to low-income and academically or physically handicapped students: Upward Bound, Talent Search, Educational Opportunity Centers, Student Support Services, Ronald

E. McNair Post-Baccalaureate Achievement Program, and Staff Training and Program Evaluation. Both Upward Bound and Talent Search reach out to students in high school. Upward Bound provides instruction in English, mathematics, and science on college campuses after school, Saturdays, and during the summer. Talent Search attempts to reduce dropout rates by helping students complete admission and financial aid applications for college. Educational Opportunity Centers provide low-income adults with information about postsecondary education opportunities. The goal of Student Support Services is to increase college graduation rates by providing tutoring, counseling, and remedial instruction. The purpose of the Ronald E. McNair Post-Baccalaureate Achievement Program, named for an astronaut killed in the 1986 space shuttle explosion, is to encourage low-income and minority undergraduates to consider careers in college teaching and to prepare them for doctoral study.

Another federal grant source, the National Science Foundation (NSF), made a commitment to strengthening the quantity and quality of minority science students by contributing $15 million in grants in FY 1992 (*Minority Funding Report* . . . , 1992). At the precollege level, the NSF is encouraging school districts with significant minority enrollments to establish partnerships with colleges and universities. There are summer science camps for junior high school students, school district projects to improve instruction, and regional centers based on a broad coalition of groups that includes school districts, colleges, businesses, state and local governments, and community organizations.

At the college level, the NSF goal is to involve undergraduate and graduate students in research. Components of the effort include early faculty mentoring, special academic counseling, and participation in research.

Some U.S. corporations have funded scholarships and fellowships for specific minority groups for particular purposes such as the following: General Motors for scholarships to Hispanic engineering students, Sears for Hispanic students, Gannet Foundation for scholarships to Hispanic journalists, IBM for minority engineering students at Tennessee State University, and General Electric with fellowships for minority professors (*Minority Funding Report* . . . , 1992).

Relatively few foundations and corporations have attempted to address the issue of campus climate. Philip Morris Companies, Ford Foundation, and the Lilly Endowment have committed more than $9 million over several years to make campus climates more tolerant (McMillen, 1992). Ford and Philip Morris have invited colleges nationwide to compete, but Lilly has restricted its awards to private colleges in eight states. Ford and Lilly look for curriculum reform and faculty development, while Philip Morris is geared toward extracurricular activities and faculty recruitment.

State governments are also concerned about assisting minority students in higher education. For example, in Illinois, the Higher Education Cooperation Act was designed to recruit and retain minority students in higher education and to facilitate the transfer of minority students from two-year to four-year institutions. For FY 1991, $3.6 million was appropriated for recruitment and retention programs and $1.25 million was appropriated for articulation grants (State of Illinois Board of Higher Education, 1990).

Elements of Successful Recruitment and Retention Programs

There is considerable literature that describes the elements of successful cultural diversity programs. Student affairs professionals should consider including some or all of the following elements in their program designs.

Recruitment Program. A well-defined recruitment program with special admission criteria designed specifically to attract minority students is a prerequisite to achieving access (Green, 1990).

Services. Services that have proved essential for retention of minority students are financial aid, career and personal counseling, academic advising, investigation of racial incidents, basic academic skills development, cooperative education, child care and transportation services, and early intervention by the student's adviser to resolve problems (Edmunds and McCurdy, 1988; Trippi and Cheatham, 1991).

Special Programs. A series of activities and events can be structured to meet the needs of minority students who experience social isolation in predominately white universities. Through these programs, minority students learn that they do not have to sacrifice their own cultural identities to become part of the general student culture (Nettles and Johnson, 1987).

Support Programs. Armstrong-West and de la Teja (1988) delineated the following support programs as particularly helpful in retaining minority students: summer "bridge," parents program, freshman orientation, mentoring, and leadership and organizational development.

Campus Climate. The academic environments should be conducive to learning for all students and should reflect, without prejudice, the reality of a pluralistic society. However, campus climates have been infected by "the proliferation of racism and the growing perception of hostility and incivility" (Henley, Powell, and Poats, 1992, p. 14).

A number of exemplary programs have been developed and implemented to counteract negative attitudes toward minority students. Gordon and Strode (1992) conducted structured telephone interviews of seven institutions that initiated programs to enhance their campus climates. States such as California, New York, and Pennsylvania have passed legislation requiring their public institutions to enact programs to address campus climate (Nayman, Resnick, and Dye, 1992).

In short, the role of external funding for cultural diversity programming seems to depend on the institutional commitment to cultural diversity programming, the availability of external sources of funding for cultural diversity programming, and the design of proposed programs. To discover the actual role of external funding for cultural diversity programming at research universities, we conducted survey research on the topic.

Survey on Funding of Cultural Diversity Programs

One purpose of the study was to collect data about the kinds of minority student programs that are offered currently at research institutions. The second goal was to discover what funding sources support existing minority student programs at research institutions, and to determine, especially, the breakdown between institutional and external funds. The third goal was to find out if minority student programming is among the top institutional priorities in research institutions. The last goal was to discern what relationship, if any, exists between the level of external funding and institutional priorities.

It was expected that research institutions would have cultural diversity programs in place and that they would be considered, in each case, an institutional priority. According to a national survey of college and university presidents conducted by the American Council on Education, presidents at research and doctoral institutions (32 percent) were more likely than their counterparts at comprehensive (21 percent), liberal arts (14 percent), and two-year colleges (5 percent) to identify interracial and intercultural relations as an area of great concern (Carnegie Foundation for the Advancement of Teaching, 1991, p. 23).

The literature did not provide any guidance in forming expectations about the use of external funding and its relationship to institutional priorities and cultural diversity programming. However, if there was strong institutional support for cultural diversity programs, we hypothesized that they would be supported with internal funding alone or with internal funding supplemented by external funding. If there was minimal institutional support for cultural diversity programs, we expected the programs to be supported entirely with external funding or with external funding supplemented by internal funding.

Method. A survey titled "Funding Minority Programming" was designed to collect data about the kinds of minority student programs offered at research institutions, the funding sources for the programs, and institutional perspectives toward externally funded programs. The survey was mailed in March 1992 to chief student affairs officers at all sixty-eight Carnegie category 1 research universities. Two weeks later, a follow-up survey was mailed. Overall, 66 percent ($N = 45$) of the recipients responded.

Approximately 70 percent of the sample worked in urban universities. Of the remaining 30 percent, approximately 18 percent worked at suburban and 12 percent at rural institutions. The average student enrollment was

23,465, and the average minority student enrollment was 4,657, or approximately 20 percent of the total student enrollment. This percentage is comparable to the 18.7 percent minority student enrollment in all institutions of higher education in 1991–1992 ("Many Colleges Report Increases . . . ," 1992). The average number of staff was 127, and the average number of minority staff was 35. Minority persons comprised approximately 28 percent of the professional staff in student affairs.

Results. Almost all of the institutions reported having a large number of student-affairs-oriented programs for minority students. Most (97.8 percent) reported special cultural events, targeted recruitment, minority scholarships, and orientation with a focus on cultural diversity; 95.6 percent sponsored summer bridge programs; 91 percent presented cross-cultural communication programming and financial assistance for minority graduate students; 88.9 percent provided leadership development training.

Faculty were involved extensively in student affairs programming for minority students: 53.3 percent of the respondents indicated that their faculties wrote joint grant proposals, 66 percent reported that their faculties coordinated special events, 73.3 percent reported that their faculties presented special conferences and workshops, and about 80 percent viewed their faculties as mentors to minority students. However, only 7 percent of the universities participating in this study required cultural diversity courses. This fact raises questions about faculty involvement in curriculum reform, which may be an appropriate topic for a future study.

The institutions varied in their commitment to programming for specific minority student populations: 93.4 percent reported that they offered programs targeted to African Americans, 80 percent for Hispanics, and 62.3 percent for Asian and Native American students. These findings may indicate institutional sensitivity to the programming needs of ethnic minority students in predominantly white institutions.

The results suggest that there is a high institutional commitment to minority student programming at U.S. research universities. Indeed, 68.9 percent of the respondents indicated that the provision of programs for minority students was included in their institutional mission statements, and 91.1 percent reported that cultural diversity was emphasized in orientation sessions for new students.

In terms of the role that external funding played in supporting cultural diversity programming, one-half of those responding indicated that 25 percent of the funding for minority student programming was supplied from external sources and believed it *should be* supplied by external funding sources. The other half indicated that all funding was and *should be* supplied by institutional funds.

The data suggest a positive relationship between high institutional commitment to minority programming and reliance on internal funding. The following percentages of institutions used internal funds only to pay program costs: summer bridge programs (69 percent), special cultural events (78 percent), orientation with a focus on cultural diversity (84 percent), targeted recruitment (87 percent), leadership development training (93 percent), and cross-cultural communication (96 percent). In addition, the following percentages of institutions supported programs for specific minority groups by internal funds alone: African American (67 percent), Hispanic (71 percent), Native American (80 percent), and Asian American (82 percent).

Also, there seems to be a positive relationship between high institutional commitment to minority programming and the use of external funds to supplement minority undergraduate scholarships: 51 percent of the respondents indicated that their institutions received external funding to supplement minority scholarships. The results do not indicate what other kinds of cultural diversity programs have been widely supplemented by external funds.

The results also suggest that most of the respondents believed that a larger role for external funding of minority student programming is appropriate. Approximately 66 percent agreed or strongly agreed that use of external funds for minority programming represented a responsible strategy to counteract budgetary constraints, and 95.6 percent believed that external organizations have a valid stake in promoting the academic success of minority students.

A clear-cut minority of respondents believed that external funding can be used more extensively. Somewhat less than one half (42.2 percent) of the respondents believed that externally funded programs were as important as internally funded programs. Further, this group, in comparison to those who responded that internally funded programs were more important, demonstrated a greater tendency to endorse the notion that external funds should play a greater role than only supporting nonpermanent programs. This group also was more likely to have had experience with state-funded programs at their institutions. In short, this group with experience in state-funded programs believed that the role of external funding should be expanded regardless of the level of institutional commitment to cultural diversity programming.

As hypothesized, cultural diversity programs were in place at most of the institutions, and cultural diversity was considered an institutional priority according to most of the respondents. With these conditions, one would expect the programs to be funded exclusively with internal funding or to be funded primarily with internal funding supplemented by external funding. The results indicate that these expectations were correct. One-half of the institutions funded their cultural diversity programs with internal funding only, and the other half funded their programs with internal funds supplemented by external funds.

Conclusion

There is an optimistic outlook for student affairs professionals who are interested in pursuing grant funding to provide support for cultural diversity programming. According to the existing literature and the results of the study of research universities reported in this chapter, cultural diversity is considered a high priority in most institutions. In addition, most institutions have developed an array of programs to address cultural diversity concerns. Moreover, funding is available from federal and state agencies and from corporate and private foundations to promote cultural diversity.

However, there is a tendency to use institutional funds to provide sole funding for cultural diversity programs. When an institution makes a major budgetary commitment to a program, it is clear that it values the program. For this reason, the majority of the respondents in our study believed that internally funded programs are more important than externally funded programs. Any consideration of other sources of funding may bring into question the level of institutional commitment to cultural diversity. In fact, one-half of the institutions in our study of research universities funded their cultural diversity programs entirely with institutional funds and believed that the programs should be funded only with internal funds.

Even though this preference for internal funding exists, we believe that institutions that value cultural diversity should consider pursuing supplementary funding to provide financial relief to beleaguered institutional budgets. Most of the chief student affairs officers in the study believed that use of external funds for minority programming represents a responsible strategy to counteract budgetary constraints. Also, almost all believed that external organizations have a valid stake in promoting the academic success of minority students.

The use of external funding as a supplement to internal funding does not constitute a reduced institutional commitment to cultural diversity. The institutions in our study still made the major contribution and commitment when only 25 percent of the program funding was supplied by an external source. In fact, one-half of the institutions in the study used approximately 75 percent internal and 25 percent external funds to support their cultural diversity programs.

Our analysis of the programs frequently funded by external sources revealed primarily scholarships and fellowships for individual undergraduate and graduate minority students. Programs such as summer bridge programs, special cultural events, focused orientation, targeted recruitment, leadership development training, and cross-cultural communication were not supplemented as often with external funding.

Student affairs professionals may want to consider areas generally supported by internal funds as well as campus climate in determining what kinds of proposals to develop. There is considerable literature that delineates the elements that lead to success in these types of programs.

Now is an appropriate time to pursue external funding for cultural diversity programming. With the goal of cultural diversity receiving widespread acceptance and the availability of a number of funding possibilities coinciding with tight institutional budgets, there is a genuine opportunity to use external sources to supplement cultural diversity programs funded primarily through institutional budgets.

References

Armstrong-West, S., and de la Teja, M. "Social and Psychological Factors Affecting the Retention of Minority Students." In M. C. Terrell and D. J. Wright (eds.), *From Survival to Success: Promoting Minority Student Retention.* Washington, D.C.: National Association of Student Personnel Administrators, 1988.

Carnegie Foundation for the Advancement of Teaching. "Perspectives on Campus Life." *Change,* Sept.-Oct. 1991, pp. 21–24.

Cheatham, H. E. "Reversing the Decline of African American Enrollment in U.S. Higher Education." *Southeastern Association of Educational Opportunity Program Personnel Journal,* 1989, 8, 14–22.

Edmunds, M. M., and McGurdy, D. P. "Academic Integration: Tools for Minority Retention." In M. C. Terrell and D. J. Wright (eds.), *From Survival to Success: Promoting Minority Student Retention.* Washington, D.C.: National Association of Student Personnel Administrators, 1988.

Gordon, S. E., and Strode, C. B. "Enhancing Cultural Diversity and Building a Climate of Understanding: Becoming an Effective Change Agent." In M. C. Terrell (ed.), *Diversity, Disunity, and Campus Community.* Washington, D.C.: National Association of Student Personnel Administrators, 1992.

Green, M. (ed.). *Minorities on Campus: A Handbook for Enhancing Diversity.* Washington, D.C.: American Council on Education, 1990.

Henley, B., Powell, T., and Poats, L. "Achieving Cultural Diversity: Meeting the Challenges." In M. C. Terrell (ed.), *Diversity, Disunity, and Campus Community.* Washington, D.C.: National Association of Student Personnel Administrators, 1992.

Jones, A. C., Terrell, M. C., and Duggar, M. "The Role of Student Affairs in Fostering Cultural Diversity in Higher Education." *NASPA Journal,* 1991, 28 (2), 121–128.

Levine, A. "The Meaning of Diversity." *Change,* Sept–Oct. 1991, pp. 4–5.

McMillen, L. "Three Grant Makers Are Awarding Millions in Effort to Improve Racial Tolerance on College Campuses." *Chronicle of Higher Education,* Feb. 26, 1992, pp. A1, A33.

"Many Colleges Report Increases in Applications for Next Fall." *Chronicle of Higher Education,* Mar. 18, 1992, p. A35.

Minority Funding Report: A Monthly Report on Federal, Private, and Nonprofit Financial Aid Opportunities for Disadvantaged and Minority Groups. East Providence, R.I.: Newsletter Press of New England, 1992

Nayman, R. L., Resnick, J. C., and Dye, R. E. "Promoting Diversity and Equity Within the California State University: System-Level Mandates, Strategies, and Issues." In M. C. Terrell (ed.), *Diversity, Disunity, and Campus Community.* Washington, D.C.: National Association of Student Personnel Administrators, 1992.

Nettles, M., and Johnson, J. "Race, Sex, and Other Determinants of College Student Socialization." *Journal of College Student Personnel,* 1987, 28, 512–524.

State of Illinois Board of Higher Education. *Higher Education Cooperation Act Fiscal Year 1991 Grant Allocations.* Springfield: State of Illinois, 1990.

Stewart, J. "Planning for Cultural Diversity: A Case Study." In H. E. Cheatham and Associates (eds.), *Cultural Pluralism on Campus*. Alexandria, Va.: American College Personnel Association Media Board, 1991.

"Trio Programs Prosper as Congress Focuses on Need for Colleges to Recruit More Low-Income Students." *Chronicle of Higher Education*, July 3, 1991, p. A17.

Trippi, J., and Cheatham, H. E. "Counseling Effects on African American College Student Graduation." *Journal of Counseling and Student Development*, 1991, 32, 342–349.

MELVIN C. TERRELL *is vice president for student affairs and professor of counselor education at Northeastern Illinois University, Chicago.*

DONNA E. RUDY *is assistant to the vice president for student affairs at Northeastern Illinois University.*

HAROLD E. CHEATHAM *is head of the Department of Counselor Education, Counseling Psychology, and Rehabilitation Services Education at The Pennsylvania State University, University Park.*

Collaboration between student affairs and institutional advancement professionals can greatly enhance efforts to involve current students in institutional advancement activities and thereby produce future donors.

Turning Students into Alumni Donors

Robbie L. Nayman, Harry R. Gianneschi, Judy M. Mandel

Previous chapters in this volume confirm the limited role that student affairs staff have had in institutional advancement activities in postsecondary education, and they acknowledge the substantive contributions student affairs involvement can make to institutional advancement efforts. In this chapter, we present the results of a recent national survey that examined both the type and depth of collaboration that currently exists between student affairs and institutional advancement offices. Specifically, the survey examined efforts to involve students in institutional advancement programs and increase student understanding and awareness of their future responsibilities as alumni donors.

Collaboration Between Student Affairs and Institutional Advancement: An Emerging Partnership

Historically, at most American colleges and universities collaboration between student affairs and university advancement staff on institutional advancement goals has been a rarity or, most often, nonexistent. In the past, mutual lack of knowledge of mission, goals, and scope of services encouraged a sense of territoriality; and the absence of occasions to interact as colleagues hampered the development of mutually beneficial working relationships between student affairs and institutional advancement staff.

As educational fundraising and institutional advancement have grown in importance as viable strategies to mitigate diminishing fiscal resources and downsizing within the higher education community, there has been increasing awareness among institutional advancement professionals of the necessity for total institutional commitment to the institutional advancement

NEW DIRECTIONS FOR STUDENT SERVICES, no. 63, Fall 1993 © Jossey-Bass Publishers

agenda. All sectors of the institution, including faculty, students, administrators, and staff, have a coordinated role to play in institutional advancement efforts if objectives are to be successfully accomplished (Evans, 1981; Shanley, 1985). Professional staff in student affairs, and in other divisions of the institution, represent untapped resources to achieve institutional advancement goals.

Similarly, chief student affairs officers are acquiring greater appreciation of the functions that institutional advancement efforts serve at today's colleges and universities in response to severe budget reductions and constraints imposed by shrinking resources. As part of the president's management team, a chief student affairs officer should be involved in strategic planning for institutional advancement activities designed to help the institution fulfill its mission and aspirations. Further, it is apparent that student affairs, and other divisions of the institution, can profit from becoming involved in institutional advancement initiatives, both to garner additional resources for their own division and for the institution as a whole.

Involving Current Students: Successful Strategies

Effective participation in alumni and institutional advancement activities by students during their undergraduate years establishes a potent foundation for future involvement with their institutions as active alumni. Much of the literature on institutional advancement activities at two- and four-year colleges and universities substantiates the importance of getting students involved with institutional advancement programs early in their college experience (Kerns, 1986; Lynch, 1980; Purpura, 1980; Shanley, 1985).

While a significant number of students felt estranged from their colleges and universities during the political turmoil of the late 1960s and mid-1970s, during the last decade there has been a resurgence of student involvement in campus activities at colleges and universities across the nation. Increasingly, institutional advancement professionals at two- and four-year public and private colleges and universities have been successful in involving students in institutional advancement activities (Todd, 1992).

Student Alumni Associations. One of the most popular and successful ways to involve current students in regular advancement activities is through the establishment of an undergraduate student alumni association. At times referred to as "university ambassadors," "student foundation," or "undergraduate educational fundraising association," these organizations, which have existed for more than fifty years (Todd, 1992), effectively socialize students into the institution's advancement culture by providing them with ample opportunities to serve in key planning and management positions.

While the nomenclature, structure, and emphases of student alumni associations are quite diverse and generally reflect the particular personalities, missions, and purposes of their respective colleges and universities, their responsibilities often include special events, campus tours, phon-a-thon educational fundraising, student giving programs, student recruitment, and community outreach. Exemplary student alumni associations are reported in the literature (Carter and Alberger, 1980; Harlan, 1980; Olson, 1992; Purpura, 1980; Todd, 1992).

Students as Financial Contributors. Students have potential as givers (Evans, 1981), and the most popular method for soliciting financial support from students in their last year before graduation is participation in a senior class gift program. Through this process, students pledge financial contributions to their colleges and universities. Various models of senior class gift and pledge programs exist throughout the education community, differing in structure, campaign timetable, size of gift, and follow-up. (For descriptions of existing models currently in operation at public and private colleges and universities, see Burdette, 1989; Carter and Alberger, 1980; Evans, 1981; Fulton, 1976; Segall, 1976.)

Students as Fundraisers. Current students have also demonstrated their effectiveness through participation in educational fundraising efforts. Student involvement in donor efforts is increasingly viewed by professionals as a method to build the "alumni habit" among students while they are still on campus (Purpura, 1980).

Successful approaches to involving students in educational fundraising efforts have been implemented at several colleges and universities across the country. At the University of Nebraska in Lincoln, current students are actively recruited into the Student Alumni Association, which encourages campus pride, involves students in collaborative educational fundraising activities with alumni, and gives recognition to the pivotal role that alumni-student relations play in drawing current students into educational fundraising activities. In the fall of 1988, the University of Nebraska at Lincoln became the national headquarters for the Student Alumni Association/Student Foundation Network, which is the umbrella organization for student alumni programs. Professional acknowledgment of this organization was given by the Council for the Advancement and Support of Education (CASE) in 1991, when CASE hired its first Student Alumni Association/Student Foundation Network intern to work in its Washington, D.C., office. As the preeminent organization for institutional advancement professionals, this endorsement of student involvement in advancement efforts had genuine significance for this student organization. Similar student alumni association chapters that recruit current students, actively engage them in campus activities, and garner financial resources for their colleges and universities can be found at Illinois State University, Indiana University, University of Rhode Island, and University of California at Berkeley (Olson, 1992), as well as at Brown University, Iowa State University, and University of Michigan (Purpura, 1980).

Another popular approach to involving students in educational fundraising is telephone solicitation. For example, at Lafayette College, students designed, managed, and staffed a phon-a-thon for a month (Evans, 1981). At California State University in Fullerton, current students are recruited by university advancement staff to participate in direct telephone solicitation for their annual fund.

Solicitation of direct support from graduating seniors in the form of senior class gift programs is widely used at colleges and universities to engage students in educational fundraising initiatives. The format and scope of these initiatives vary considerably. There is the "5X" plan at Texas Christian University in which graduating seniors pledge to give $5 before graduation and to increase their gifts by at least $5 each year thereafter (Segall, 1976). At Skidmore College, the senior class gift represents a strong tradition of campus culture, and each graduating class approaches its senior class gift as a part of the overall institutional advancement effort at the college.

Students can enhance overtures to corporate and foundation donors for financial support of academic programs and student cocurriculum activities. In some settings, students can be included when prospective donors are visited.

Key Student Constituent Groups. Some colleges and universities re-cruit students to educational fundraising efforts through appeals to their unique interests and needs in terms of gender, ethnicity, and social affil-iations (Lewis, 1981; Seiple, 1981). Thus, student constituent groups such as women, minority students, older students, and Greeks can be introduced to institutional advancement efforts and invited to participate in their implementation.

Student Leadership and Community Service Programs

Positive public relations are essential for effective advancement efforts on behalf of an institution. Increasingly, as community service has become recognized as an effective vehicle for contributing to the common good and enabling students to gain valuable leadership experiences, institutional advancement and student affairs professionals have begun to explore how student involvement in community service programs helps advancement efforts by garnering good public relations for their institutions.

Diffily (1989) suggested that community service initiatives and institu-tional advancement activities can be combined to attract student participa-tion and enhance the public relations of the nation's colleges and universities. A promising example of this approach is Campus Compact and its Student Humanitarian Awards program. Campus Compact, established in 1985 by the presidents of Brown University, Georgetown University, and Stanford University, is a national coalition of college and university presidents committed to promoting civic responsibility and student volunteerism on campus. The student humanitarian awards of Campus Compact have enabled colleges and universities to showcase their public service contributions to their communities, spotlight exemplary student projects, and thereby enhance the public relations dimension of institutional advancement efforts.

Sample and Methodology of a National Survey

To probe the scope, strategies, and constraints of collaboration between student affairs and institutional advancement professionals for involving students in alumni and institutional advancement programs, we mailed questionnaires to a random sample of 545 members of the National Association of Student Personnel Administrators (NASPA) and CASE during the fall semester of 1991. The sample was drawn from these two organizations because NASPA is the largest national organization of student personnel administrators and, similarly, CASE is the professional organization with which the majority of institutional advancement professionals are affiliated.

The survey focused on institutional advancement activities for students then currently enrolled, since most alumni and institutional advancement activities have traditionally been designed for graduating seniors and recent graduates, with relatively scant attention devoted to lower-division college students. The survey response rate was 61 percent. Respondents were nearly equally divided between student affairs staff (49.7 percent) and institutional advancement staff (50.3 percent) and represented three institutional sectors: public four-year colleges and universities (47.3 percent), private four-year colleges and universities (46.1 percent), and community colleges (6.6 percent).

The same questionnaire was mailed to chief student affairs and institutional advancement officers. The questionnaire was designed to determine the dimensions of professional relationships perceived to exist between these two units of the college or university. The specific areas that the questionnaire explored were involvement of student affairs and institutional advancement staffs in student programs for alumni and institutional advancement efforts, institutional support for collaboration, scope of activities undertaken collaboratively for current students, attitudes toward collaborative efforts between these two units of the institution, and mutual areas of concern related to existing and potential collaboration.

Findings of the Survey

The emerging relationship between student affairs and institutional advancement faces a number of challenges and opportunities, as indicated by the findings in this national survey of professionals from the two units.

Student Programs: Involvement of Student Affairs and Institutional Advancement. Student affairs and institutional advancement respondents from private and public colleges and universities and from community colleges reported that they provided activities and programs involving current students in alumni and institutional advancement efforts. In response to the question "Does your institution have student programs devoted to development activities?" the largest percentage of respondents who answered yes were from private colleges and universities (73 percent), reflecting the history of voluntary support and tradition of philanthropy toward American private education. In contrast, 56 percent of respondents from public colleges and universities and 32 percent of respondents from community colleges described institutional advancement programs for students, which is consistent with the relatively recent emphasis on institutional advancement efforts within these two institutional sectors.

The involvement of student affairs and institutional advancement in student programs was also examined from the perspective of whether student programs were included in the yearly goals of each area. They were included in 48 percent of institutional advancement goals but in only 32 percent of student affairs goals. This finding reflects the recency of student affairs movement toward substantive involvement in advancement programs and activities.

Turning students into donors is a socialization process that involves orienting students to the notion of voluntary giving, actively engaging them in varied institutional advancement activities, and strategically timing program initiatives. In the present study, respondents were asked if they sponsored programs directed at informing students about their future role as alumni: 52 percent of respondents from private colleges and universities offered such programs, while only 29.4 percent of respondents from public colleges and universities and 14 percent of community college respondents offered these programs.

Scope of Collaboration Between Student Affairs and Institutional Advancement. Currently, collaboration on student programs between student affairs and institutional advancement is modest. The limited character of joint efforts, regardless of institutional type, was apparent in the responses to the question of whether the two areas currently assisted each other with programs to encourage student participation in educational fundraising. Respondents from private and public colleges and universities and from community colleges all responded no in similar numbers (71 percent, 76 percent, and 73 percent, respectively). When this question was analyzed by type of respondents, student affairs respondents and institutional advancement respondents did not significantly differ in their responses.

As part of this question, student affairs and institutional advancement respondents were asked to describe joint efforts between their areas. Numerous descriptions of such efforts were prefaced with or followed by qualifiers such as "limited to," "mostly informal," "if we ask them," "only on specific limited basis," "just starting," and "to a limited degree." These qualifiers suggest circumscribed rather than truly collaborative relationships. Despite the relatively modest number of respondents who reported joint efforts, the range of collaborative efforts undertaken between student affairs and institutional advancement was impressive: phon-a-thons, annual telethons, graduation picnics, career networks and workshops, senior class fund drives, parents associations, internships, senior banquets, student foundations, senior challenge campaigns, alumni ambassadors, pre-alumni council advisement, homecoming weekends, career days for alumni, scholarship programs, student ambassador programs, and student alumni associations.

Protracted fiscal crises and retrenchment of staff may be mitigating factors in the degree of collaboration between student affairs and institutional advancement offices, besides the equally challenging issue of attitude barriers that may exist due to lack of mutual familiarity with professional expertise between the two groups. Respondents were asked if their areas had staff with assigned responsibility for student programs devoted to educational fundraising: 55 percent of institutional advancement respondents answered yes, compared to 20 percent of student affairs respondents.

Perceptions of Collaboration Between Student Affairs and Institutional Advancement. Prevailing perceptions and attitudes among student affairs and institutional advancement professionals regarding collaborative efforts are, in general, decisive factors in achieving effective working relationships. Several questions in our survey explored attitudes toward collaboration and strategies for increasing student participation in institutional advancement activities.

On a scale of 1 (strongly disagree) to 5 (strongly agree), respondents from private and public colleges and universities and from community colleges responded at a level between "neutral" and "agree" to the questionnaire item concerning collegiality between student affairs and institutional advancement staff at their institutions, and the three groups did not differ from one another in their levels of agreement on that item ($F[154] = 2.18$, n.s.). Private college and university respondents disagreed less ($M = 2.23$) than did respondents from public colleges and universities ($M = 1.87$) and community colleges ($M = 1.82$) on the statement concerning whether students understood the role of private giving ($F[2,157] = 3.83, p < .03$). Disagreement with this item was greatest among public four-year institution and community college respondents, reflecting the ethos of private colleges and universities and their culture of voluntary support.

The task of involving current students in institutional advancement programs and activities to create future donors "competes" for staff attention and resources with other facets of alumni and institutional advancement priorities. The degree of priority given to establishing programs that get students involved in institutional advancement efforts early in their collegiate experience, both by student affairs and institutional advancement professionals, ultimately influences the likelihood of greater collaboration between these two groups. To gauge the status given to student programs, respondents were asked to rate their divisions' success in providing programs that involved current students in educational fundraising. While perceptions of success differed according to institutional context, the overall rating of success was modest. Community colleges rated their success lowest, whereas private schools provided the highest rating of perceived success. Perceptions of limited success in providing programs that get current students involved in institutional advancement may mirror consequences of the practice of emphasizing student programs for seniors and recent alumni, as opposed to providing programs for current students early in their collegiate experience. Another finding in this study was that very few respondents at four-year institutions reported offering programs before the students' senior year of college.

Salient Issues in Involving Current Students in Institutional Advancement Activities. The lack of parity of institutional advancement activities for current students or recent alumni compared with other aspects of educational fundraising and institutional advancement is one of the most compelling issues facing the nation's colleges and universities. As a profession, institutional advancement is still in the process of coming of age and defining its constituent components, which are in competition with one another on some campuses (Pray, 1981a). Indeed, "the development profession is still in the process of integrating and consolidating the evolutionary changes that brought it into being" (Pray, 1981b, p. 389).

Other key issues were reflected in the comments made by respondents. Student affairs and institutional advancement respondents were asked to include any final observations regarding joint efforts between the two units to develop students as donors. Comments by student affairs professionals included the following: "Though I recognize the need to develop future donors among our current student bodies, I think timing is important. Developmentally, junior and senior year is early enough, in my opinion, to begin encouraging students to think about support for their alma mater." "Educational fundraising is definitely not a goal of our student affairs division, nor do we want it to be." "We are glad to work with the institutional advancement office in this effort, but we are wary of any student affairs enterprise becoming an 'educational fundraising' event." Comments by institutional advancement professionals included the following: "We would like to be involved in efforts to orient and educate students but there are more pressing needs with larger, swifter results from actions that are taken." "There are many priorities in institutional advancement . . . most with greater short-term giving potential than student institutional advancement programs." "Good area to study. I believe we can make linkages of greater impact when faculty are involved in promoting giving rather than student affairs staffs." "Having been in student affairs prior to institutional advancement, I am disappointed at both sides of the institution for not providing a stronger commitment for the role and responsibilities each plays." The volume and diversity of opinions proffered illuminate substantive issues that warrant thoughtful reflection, for they likely forecast challenges to achieving future collaboration between student affairs and institutional advancement, and to fully harnessing the potential contributions current students are capable of making to their colleges and universities.

Implications for Future Collaboration

Providing students opportunities to participate in activities that offer growth experiences and enable them to contribute through their participation in programs that assist their colleges and universities is the basic premise for student involvement in institutional advancement programs. Such programs will be greatly enhanced and more efficiently delivered if student affairs and institutional advancement professionals function as colleagues who have mutual knowledge of each other's mission, goals, and services.

References

Burdette, M. "Cooking Up a Senior Gift Program." *CASE Currents,* 1989, *15* (2), 14–18.

Carter, V., and Alberger, P. A. (eds.). *Building Your Alumni Program: The Best of CASE Currents.* Washington, D.C.: Council for the Advancement and Support of Education, 1980. (ED 192 697)

Diffily, A. H. "Making the Ideal Real." *CASE Currents,* 1989, *15* (2), 6–13.

Evans, G. "Student Fund Raisers and Contributors." In F. C. Pray (ed.), *Handbook for Educational Fund Raising: A Guide to Successful Principles and Practices for Colleges, Universities, and Schools.* San Francisco: Jossey-Bass, 1981.

Fulton, G. "A Gift That Keeps Giving." *CASE Currents,* 1976, *2* (11), 8.

Harlan, W. "How to Start a Student Alumni Organization." *Student Alumni Association and Foundations,* 1980, *6* (10), 4–6.

Kerns, J. R. "Two-Year College Alumni Programs into the 1990s." Paper presented at the National Workshop on Two-Year College Alumni Programs, Junior and Community College Institute, Washington, D.C., June 1986. (ED 277 435)

Lewis, F. "Older Students as Volunteers and Informal Advisers." In F. C. Pray (ed.), *Handbook for Educational Fund Raising: A Guide to Successful Principles and Practices for Colleges, Universities, and Schools.* San Francisco: Jossey-Bass, 1981.

Lynch, H. G. "The Young Alumnus: An Enduring Strength." In V. Carter and P. A. Alberger (eds.), *Building Your Alumni Program: The Best of CASE Currents.* Washington, D.C.: Council for the Advancement and Support of Education, 1980. (ED 192 697)

Olson, B. "SASs: The Student's View." *CASE Currents,* 1992, *18* (5), 9–10.

Pray, F. C. (ed.). *Handbook for Educational Fund Raising: A Guide to Successful Principles and Practices for Colleges, Universities, and Schools.* San Francisco: Jossey-Bass, 1981a.

Pray, F. C. "Trends in Institutional Resource Management." In F. C. Pray (ed.), *Handbook for Educational Fund Raising: A Guide to Successful Principles and Practices for Colleges, Universities, and Schools.* San Francisco: Jossey-Bass, 1981b.

Purpura, M. "Building the ALUMNI HABIT." In V. Carter and P. A. Alberger (eds.), *Building Your Alumni Program: The Best of CASE Currents.* Washington, D.C.: Council for the Advancement and Support of Education, 1980. (ED 192 697)

Segall, L. "Start That Habit Early: Senior Giving 5X." *CASE Currents,* 1976, *2* (10), 5–6. (ED 177 931)

Seiple, C. "Women as Givers and Getters." In F. C. Pray (ed.), *Handbook for Educational Fund Raising: A Guide to Successful Principles and Practices for Colleges, Universities, and Schools.* San Francisco: Jossey-Bass, 1981.

Shanley, M. G. "Student, Faculty and Staff Involvement in Institutional Advancement: University of South Carolina." *Carolina View,* 1985, *1,* 40–43. (ED 272 133)

Todd, B. T. "Uniting to Improve Student-Alumni Relations." *CASE Currents,* 1992, *18* (5), 10.

ROBBIE L. NAYMAN *is vice president for student affairs at California State University, Fullerton.*

HARRY R. GIANNESCHI *is vice president for university advancement at California State University, Fullerton.*

JUDY M. MANDEL *is director of special giving at California State University, Fullerton.*

Chief student affairs officers should play a leadership role in institutional advancement activities because, as members of the top-level administrative team, they help determine how to implement institutional missions and strategic plans. Therefore, student affairs administrators should include institutional advancement activities in their job descriptions.

The Challenge of Chief Student Affairs Officers: Planning for the Future

James A. Gold, Dennis C. Golden, Thomas J. Quatroche

Today, all administrators seek optimal services to their students, strict adherence to institutional mission and goals, and prudent investment in the human and material capital required for the college or university's very survival and growth. Institutional advancement activity creates goodwill. It brings dollars into the institution, but it also enables administrators to tell the community what their institution represents.

It is not surprising that the student affairs unit is among the most financially vulnerable in an era of reduction (Williamson and Mamarchev, 1990). It is often identified and evaluated as supportive and sometimes as nonessential to the primary educational aims of the institution. Under the most austere circumstances, it may become viewed as tangential rather than integral to these aims.

These political realities give the chief student affairs officer (CSAO) pause, because student affairs staff are expected to continue operating at a high level of proficiency when the overall institution is fiscally threatened. Thus, when internal budget restrictions threaten pernicious consequences for the delivery and quality of student services, the student affairs units must turn more frequently to external educational fundraising as a remedy.

Role of the Vice President

Historically, CSAOs have played a nominal role, if involved at all, in the educational fundraising endeavors of their institutions. Educational fundraising has been regarded as chiefly within the exclusive domains of presidents and institutional advancement officers. However, in consider-

New Directions for Student Services, no. 63, Fall 1993 © Jossey-Bass Publishers

ation of the growing need for alternative external funding sources, CSAOs more keenly recognize the essential role educational fundraising can play in the planning and operation of the student affairs unit. Moreover, they realize that additional resources will not be forthcoming unless they assertively adopt a leadership role in the educational fundraising enterprise.

Arguments supporting the CSAO's involvement in institutional advancement activities have been recently espoused (Sandeen, 1991, pp. 33–36). Vital knowledge about the student and the student's family, including their location, professional achievements, and status, is welcomed by the chief institutional advancement officer (CIAO). It makes sense for CSAOs to expand their activity base beyond the traditional role in student services and programs. Educational fundraising is a high-visibility activity. If tied to institutional mission, any success is quickly acknowledged and appreciated by the campus president and key faculty leaders.

The CSAO enhances his or her portfolio through institutional advancement and educational fundraising activities by creating more frequent opportunities to associate with alumni, the president, and other campus leaders, thus influencing the priorities of the institution for the future. Can we support an academic chair for a notable writer, teacher, or researcher on the U.S. college student who can simultaneously affirm the role of student affairs staff as influential agents of student growth? The presence of a visiting chair for just a few months might change the institution and the relationship of student affairs to it in dramatically positive ways.

The student affairs staff can provide considerable information about potential prospects, their backgrounds or connections to the institution, and even their capacity and willingness to give. Student affairs staff are critical as partners in the actual solicitation process.

Kroll (1991) has provided the most definitive statement on the evolving role of student affairs officers in academic educational fundraising. Her comprehensive survey of presidents, institutional advancement officers, and CSAOs at small liberal arts colleges found an expanding role for student affairs staff in educational fundraising and institutional advancement activities. While student affairs officers are adopting more of the role behavior of other institutional officers, nowhere is the trend more pronounced than in their adoption of the role of the institutional advancement officer. The maturing of the student affairs profession appears to have a strong institutional advancement component.

Hence, it is generally accepted in the present financial climate that the CSAO must incorporate educational fundraising as a central component in the planning and operation of the student affairs unit. What is not so clear to most CSAOs is how best to achieve educational fundraising objectives. Counterpoised to the newly prevailing consensus that educational fundraising is an imperative is the scarcity of literature on how to fundraise from a student affairs perspective.

The American College Personnel Association Commission I report *Task*

Force on Alternative Sources of Funding for Student Affairs Programs (Patterson, 1992) showed that most of the external funding was from government sources. The two leading sources were the Fund for the Improvement of Postsecondary Education and federal Title III monies. Although the subject areas included alcohol and other drug abuse prevention, retention, counseling, health and wellness issues, multicultural diversity, disabled student programs, and peer advising, the vast majority of the funding came as part of other institutional grants and seldom for the sole purpose of student affairs.

Without the benefit of substantial research or apparent institutional paradigms, where does the uninitiated CSAO begin to formulate a strategy for effective educational fundraising? The process must begin with awareness of and confidence in the vital role and influence of student services on the achievement of the institution's unique mission and goals. The second step is to place educational fundraising within its proper framework as an essential executive responsibility. Educational fundraising is no longer a peripheral activity in most institutions of higher education. It is a central institutional activity that functions consistently with the overall mission.

Educational Fundraising Plan

The task of putting together a convincing educational fundraising plan that conforms to the specific concerns of the campus involves careful research into the implications of the educational fundraising goals within the context of the overall mission and strategic plan of the institution. How will these enhancements advance the institution's mission and goals? How will they affect enrollment management? How will the goals of the fund drive accommodate the needs of the surrounding community? And does this project respond to demographic changes, perhaps ultimately altering the composition of the student body?

The CSAO must be prepared to answer the multiple questions stemming from the exclusive attributes, expectations, and levels of influence of each constituent group. The answers provided must reflect, reiterate, and reinforce the fundamental ideological and pragmatic framework in which institutional policy is formulated and implemented. As much as each institution possesses its own distinct character, each master plan must represent what is unique about the groups that it addresses. Thus, a convincing educational fundraising plan addresses the interests and concerns of the constituencies that it is designed to serve, and it encompasses the mission or the strategic plan of the college or university as a whole.

Leadership

Leadership is the one role played by the CSAO that more than any other influences the success of the educational fundraising process in student affairs. Should professional institutional advancement officers join the student affairs team? Fundraisers and grant preparation specialists are seldom, if ever, assigned to student services projects, and whatever is accomplished gets done because of general productivity gains by traditional student affairs personnel. "Having a fund raising staff person in the student affairs division may have a special promise for development efforts targeted to specific capital projects, such as unions, residence halls, or recreation buildings" (Sandeen, 1991, p. 36).

Setting the Leadership Stage

It is important that the CSAO, to be clearly recognized as a leader in institutional advancement activities, work within an institutional framework that supersedes his or her personality or career ambition and that in no way diverts essential energies from the functions of student services. That is why the job description of the CSAO *must* be rewritten to include educational fundraising.

Power-coercive strategies should not be used by the CSAO in an educational fundraising initiative, which could be scuttled by lower-level student affairs staff who may not see the need for change, particularly if their essential role in serving students is diverted. There must be a well-understood benefit to all participants, thus increasing the probability of success. According to Creamer and Creamer (1990), success depends more on collaboration and facilitation than the strong visionary behavior of a leader. Leader charisma may be short-lived when an organizational change as complex as fund development is introduced.

A general approach to planning for the future of educational fundraising programs in student affairs requires answers to the following questions:

What is the specific vision for the future of a successful educational fundraising program?

What are the practical assigned roles to accomplish the plan?

What are the limiting factors, barriers, hurdles, and deterrents to the achievement of the vision?

What are the major changes or programs that can be developed to overcome barriers to realizing an effective educational fundraising program?

What are the major goals to be set and actions that must be taken in the next year to implement the plan, and who is responsible for continuous improvements in the plan?

How will the CSAO award those who achieve?

Is there a coalition of supporters both within and outside of student affairs who can help ensure the success of new educational fundraising initiatives?

Can student affairs staff be sufficiently educated in the politically sensitive arena of educational fundraising?

Will this education include an understanding of the risks of venturing into unknown territory, where the visible consequences of failure can severely alienate other powerful figures within and outside the institution?

Can the educational fundraising plan be modified along the way to take into account the concerns of strongly negative stakeholders who may subvert these new initiatives?

Can counterarguments be prepared in advance for those individuals who require rapprochement to gain their support?

The President

A CSAO has a limited constituency. A campus president has a complete constituency and thus is the diviner of the mission of the institution. An awkward CSAO seeking aggrandizement through spectacular educational fundraising results will not survive long. The mission and values of the institution must be the backdrop against which all student affairs functions are actualized, most especially functions that are the primary assignment of another executive officer or officers.

As Shay (this volume) points out, the key to initiating a successful institutional advancement program for student affairs lies in a supportive relationship with the CIAO and the campus president. Since a close working relationship with these two individuals is critical, it makes sense to carefully think out the entire process before approaching them. One must anticipate direct and indirect resistance from these two officers, whose own success depends on their stewardship of potential donors with whom the CSAO is proposing to interact at some level.

"Student affairs administrators generally have not been adept in understanding and using the political processes of higher education. The skill deficit must be corrected if student affairs is to be an equal partner in the future of higher education of the community" (Barr and Albright, 1990, pp. 191–192). This may be one reason why presidents are hesitant to tap their CSAOs as potential fundraisers.

Important linkages must be established between the internal and external environments of student affairs, on the one hand, and other segments of the institution and the wider community of potential donors, on the other hand. The CSAO's challenge is to establish these linkages in ways that appeal to the campus president. The CSAO must obtain the sanction and commitment of all the primary players in educational fundraising and be prepared to rebut any claims of the nonprimacy of educational fundraising as a decreed student affairs activity.

Being Realistic

To obtain additional resources for the student affairs division, the CSAO's vision of success must be, above all, realistic. Lofty speculation about new resources, deluxe facilities, ample funds for staff institutional advancement, and easy social access to important, powerful, and rich members of the community will quickly give way to feelings of frustration, disenchantment, and regressive backbiting by a crestfallen and discouraged staff.

Success depends on a realistic vision combined with appropriate actions. If clear-cut procedures and actions do not follow from the success vision, then all good intentions will be turned to ruin. The preferred scenario is to achieve educational fundraising results without calling away student affairs staff from the salutary provision of direct services to students. It is important to help staff recognize the perils to a successful educational fundraising experience long before initiatives are set in motion. They may then be prepared to surmount those hazards and achieve objectives without rancor or division.

Strategic Planning

What is strategic planning and why is it so critical? Strategic planning is a visionary process that enables the administrator to establish priorities and set a course toward efficiently managed resources. Also, it prevents organizational conflict, a most essential goal for the effective administrator.

Since Keller's (1983) book on academic strategy, there has been a steady emphasis on the application of management planning strategies to all aspects of higher education. But perhaps the greatest success has been achieved in the area of educational fundraising by both public and private sector institutions.

Strategic planning offers new opportunities to reach agreement across organizational units and boundaries and to regularly create and modify institutional strategies for action. "Higher education has experienced a managerial transformation in the 1980s characterized by an increased emphasis on financial planning, enrollment management, marketing, strategic planning, and computer technology" (Schuh and Rickard, 1989, p. 462). Most CSAOs apply strategic market planning principles to maximize resources and take advantage of new opportunities (Rea and Rea, 1990). The same approach can serve educational fundraising objectives.

Strategic planning is initiated with the creation of a mission statement. The sense of purpose gained through a clear mission statement is vital. "Ultimately, strategic planning is about purpose, meaning, values, and virtue, and nowhere is this more apparent than in the clarification of mission and the subsequent development of a vision of success" (Bryson, 1988, p. 96). It is not enough to generate clarity through a mission statement. It is also essential to generate excitement. Bryson (1988, p. 48) described an eight-step strategic planning process: (1) initiating and agreeing on a strategic planning process, (2) identifying organizational mandates, (3) clarifying organizational mission and values, (4) assessing the external environment: opportunities and threats, (5) assessing the internal environment: strengths and weaknesses, (6) identifying the strategic issues facing an organization, (7) formulating strategies to manage the issues, and (8) establishing an effective organizational vision for the future.

Clarification of an organization's mission and values is the surest way to guarantee consensus on an educational fundraising role for the student affairs division. The overarching mission of an institution is its reason for existence and gives all members within the campus community a clear purpose. Vital organizations continue to redefine themselves not by changing their missions but by attending carefully to that mission while the environment within the institution creates new pressures on it. Challenges and opportunities in actualizing the mission are always faced.

Strategic Issues

The task of identifying strategic issues around the mounting and delivery of a successful institutional advancement program involves sizing up the clarity of institutional mission, the means for achieving problematic goals, the details involved in who is accountable for achieving results, and the proposed remedies for likely problems and failures. The identification of strategic issues involves the identification of solutions to real and anticipated problems. Failure to anticipate problems can invoke a whole series of political conflicts that will seriously drain energy, if not resources, from essential student services. Additionally, conflict-of-interest issues, ethical and moral issues, and basic fiscal accountability and record-keeping procedures must be considered.

Formulation of successful strategies to manage institutional advancement issues must be broad-based, highly participatory, and creative in the presentation of choices and actions across many institutional units and individuals. Multiple strategies to solve problems and capitalize on opportunities will pay real dividends as student affairs staff enter this relatively unfamiliar arena. An honest early appraisal of barriers to successful goal achievement can help the CSAO avoid tragic organizational conflicts, minimize false starts, and reduce potential morale problems resulting from the lack of expertise of student affairs staff in educational fundraising.

Centralization

To effectively fundraise, one must be aware of legal issues, conflict-of-interest problems, and the need for protection of confidential information and authorization to negotiate. Attention to these matters requires greater centralization of policy and procedure than some student affairs staff are willing to tolerate. Most student affairs staff prefer a decentralized approach to the organization and supervision of their work. They highly value individual staff freedom and autonomy and possess a strong desire to be spontaneous and individually responsive to their various constituencies, especially when directly serving students.

However, there is simply no substitute for centralized educational fundraising services, including data and process analysis, budget development, and even day-to-day management (Hardy, 1991). Educational fundraising requires the use of computers and sophisticated techniques such as geodemographic analysis. Proficiency in designing surveys, collecting retention data, leading focus groups, and using data services results in efficient student or donor prospect groupings (Crane, 1991). Centralization is a necessary adjunct to competent educational fundraising.

Planning Committee

A permanent strategic planning committee composed of student affairs directors and key personnel can provide the essential planning and evaluation functions necessary to sustain a self-monitoring educational fundraising process. Regular meetings between this group and key players outside student affairs must be the principal effort of the CSAO, who in most cases directs the strategic planning.

Troubleshooting the Planning Process

Before and during the planning process, it makes sense to be aware of a number of pitfalls. Be alert to the following questions:

Is it possible to achieve a consensus on goals for student affairs that are consistent with the institutional mission?

Is the institution's mission specific enough to offer a framework within which student affairs can take its place among other important institutional priorities?

Is the trust level high among top campus administrators, and are agendas above board?

If vested interests are present, is there a general consensus on priorities?

How open is the president and the CIAO to changing goals and incorporating a student affairs point of view?

Is the student affairs division prepared to incorporate educational fundraising as a basic value?

Are there sufficient numbers and adequately trained student affairs staff to represent a total planning group?

Is the planning group capable of handling the inevitable conflict that occurs whenever a major educational fundraising effort is undertaken?

Is there need for a new or modified organizational structure to achieve educational fundraising objectives?

Would a new planning structure create jurisdictional problems among the established student affairs leadership team?

Will there be adequate representation across all student affairs areas, or just a special few?

What will be the limitations on planning efforts?

How much information will be shared among student affairs staff, and by what means?

Will the plan be subject to widespread or limited feedback, evaluation, and revision?

On whose shoulders will fall the responsibility for the accuracy and comprehensiveness of data?

What will be the relationship of the planning group to line staff?

How will the planning team interact with units and subunits within the student affairs division?

What will be the cost of the planning, execution, and evaluation of the educational fundraising effort?

Who will determine the reallocation of divisional resources?

How much of all of the above will be centralized or decentralized among the units in the student affairs division, and how will rewards for successful efforts be allocated?

Developing a Constituency

Potential donors can be depicted as the hub of a wheel around which spokes go to family, career, religion, education, recreation, politics, and social activities (Rosso, 1991, pp. 36–38). Fundraisers who attempt to establish connections with a potential donor based on one or more of these important roles and responsibilities will improve the chances of creating a successful kinship with this individual. Prospects who can be pulled to the institution via several of these connecting roles and responsibilities will bond to the institutional mission.

Since individual student affairs departments will be assessing their own needs for additional resources, they will be especially motivated to uncover potential donor sources. By working in a coordinated framework with other student affairs staff and the institutional advancement office, it will be possible to appropriate donors. A mutual blending of staff skills and institutional priorities will take place.

In some cases, direct contact between student affairs staff and potential donors can be problematic. For example, if student affairs staff have liberal political opinions and a potential donor complains about the publicized student protests connected with corporate America or military spending, the donor may be challenged and put on the defensive by a remonstrative student affairs staff person. No surprise, donors with opposing political opinions are sensitive about giving their money to an institution that supports or condones such student behavior.

Targeting Alumni

Institutional priorities need to be accurately conveyed to potential donors, including graduates and their families. Institutional researchers on student affairs staffs are well positioned to obtain new information about student attitudes, characteristics, activities, and goals.

Institutional advancement officers have capitalized on the "small is better" philosophy of student organizations and groups. We know that students identify with units within the institution, whether academic departments, clubs, organizations, or athletic teams. So most donor telephone solicitations now are tied to knowledge of the subunit memberships of alumni, at least by category of academic major. Student affairs staff can fill in the gaps regarding other activities and memberships.

Donor Involvement

Because the college or university is a community, many donors nostalgically seek a reconnection to the idealism that they experienced in their early years. Donors who never attended college are even more idyllic in their images of the college experience. The popularity of summer continuing education and personal institutional advancement programs can be partially explained by the remembrance of a caring and supportive campus community. These linkages to the community and alumni outside the campus are extremely valuable for fundraisers. However, there are many questions that must be answered before an aggressive program of donor involvement is pursued:

What are the most promising institutional opportunities to which donors can become connected?

How do donors get involved?

To what extent are student affairs staff involved in the prioritizing of such involvement?

How can student ambassadors encourage and support donor involvement in campus-based clubs, organizations, and advisory committees?

Do institutional policies and practices induce donor involvement in campus activities and programs?

How might donors be made to feel welcome at special campus events?

How are donors to be invited by students, faculty, and administrators?

Who follows up after donors have participated?

To what extent are underrepresented students involved in these activities?

What leadership roles can be provided for female faculty and staff to develop a constituent base?

How are Greek organizations encouraged to perform in ways consistent with the institutional mission?

How is the CIAO assisted in learning about student life on the campus?

Is the quality of student life a highly valued interest of the CIAO and the campus president?

Do students, faculty, and staff have a shared vision of the institution and its activities?

What are the characteristics of students coming into contact with potential donors?

Is there a careful match between donors and students?

How might the activities of students and other members of the campus community be explained to donors in ways that anticipate objections to, for example, the political liberalism apparent in some student and faculty actions?

In what ways does the CSAO "prepare" students to interact with potential donors, trustees, and other powerful persons in the community?

Critical Information

There are useful, if not vital, types of educational fundraising information that can be collected, organized, analyzed, and applied in the process of making strategic decisions about the implementation of a comprehensive educational fundraising program. As many of the following questions as practical should be considered when sizing up the information system:

How well is the institutional advancement office—its procedures, information base, and connections—known throughout the organization?

Is there a system in place to utilize every staff member as an information gatherer?

Has everyone been made a fundraiser?

Is there a system in place for collecting and presenting all useful information obtained by members of the organization concerning the educational fundraising process, including donor prospects, contacts, and follow-up activities?

Are the staff members "intuitive listeners" in relation to prospective donors, with the ability and interest needed to truly appreciate the motives, needs, and reactions of the potential donors to the institution?

Is there ready information available on the organization, including descriptive fact sheets, articles about special events and programs, statistics on students served, and plans for the future?

The Annual Fund

Of all the opportunities to fundraise, the most productive means for acquiring resources is through the annual fund. Student affairs staff typically are adroit in connecting with individuals who have a special relationship to the institution. "The annual fund is the building block for all educational fund raising. . . . The annual fund is the cornerstone and the key to success for all aspects of the resources development program" (Rosso, 1991, p. 51).

Solicitation

Student affairs can be extraordinarily successful in providing a stable base of capable volunteers, especially student volunteers, to provide leadership and to encourage students to be fundraisers. Student telephone banks are widely used. Givers are especially responsive to students who make a strong case for the institution. Students are often the only persons able to approach potential givers. It is harder to turn down a student than a professional fundraiser. Students who are well trained and informed can also provide continuing testimony to the benefit of money previously given.

Advisories

Boards and councils should be in place to support the efforts of individual departments and program coordinators. These advisory councils, committees, or support groups may be included in educational fundraising. While the campus president may not have direct control over these organizations, he or she should be invited to welcome the groups, speak about the state of the institution, and in other ways affirm gifts of time, energy, and ideas.

Staff Development

There may be signals of reticence by staff to become involved in educational fundraising activities. This reticence should be respected. Some staff simply do not have the time, inclination, or initial ability to see the relevance of educational fundraising for students or for their own specialized areas. The "what's-in-it-for-me?" question will eventually need to be answered. Many student affairs goals have fundraising implications. We have already discussed student educational fundraising, but there is also the need to attract and retain students. There is the need to provide community support for the college—not just political or public relations support but the support of solicited dollars.

Student affairs staff do have adaptive abilities that enable them to conduct educational fundraising activities. We need to nurture these talents and help them to expand their educational fundraising involvement. Transferable talents from student affairs work to educational fundraising activities include people skills, community-building skills, personal growth orientation, leadership capability, counseling and mediation skills, and ability to convey enthusiasm for the institution.

References

Barr, M. J., and Albright, R. L. "Rethinking the Organizational Role of Student Affairs." In M. J. Barr, M. L. Upcraft (eds.), *New Futures for Student Affairs*. San Francisco: Jossey-Bass, 1990.

Bryson, J. M. *Strategic Planning for Public and Nonprofit Organizations: A Guide to Strengthening and Sustaining Organizational Achievement*. San Francisco: Jossey-Bass, 1988.

Crane, P. "A Tool, Not a Magic Wand: The Limits of Geodemographics." *CASE Currents*, 1991, 17 (4), 46–47.

Creamer, D. G., and Creamer, E. G. "Use of a Planned Change Model to Modify Student Affairs Programs." In D. G. Creamer and Associates, *College Student Development: Theory and Practice for the 1990s*. Media Publication No. 49. Alexandria, Va.: American College Personnel Association Media Board, 1990.

Hardy, R. "Strategic Advancement: How a Centralized Services Department Can Do More Than Support Fund Raisers." *CASE Currents*, 1991, 17 (6), 20–23.

Keller, G. *Academic Strategy: The Management Revolution in American Higher Education*. Baltimore: Johns Hopkins University Press, 1983.

Kroll, D. N. "Role Expansion in Student Affairs: Student Affairs Officers and Fund Raising in Selected Midwestern Liberal Arts Colleges." Unpublished doctoral dissertation, Ohio State University, 1991.

Patterson, J. L. *Task Force on Alternative Sources of Funding for Student Affairs Programs: Final Report*. Washington, D.C.: Commission I, American College Personnel Association, 1992.

Rea, P. J., and Rea, J. S. "Strategic Market Planning: A Useful Tool for Career Services and Recruiting Offices." *Journal of Career Planning and Employment*, 1990, 51 (1), 41–46.

Rosso, H. A. "Developing a Constituency: Where Fund Raising Begins." In H. A. Rosso and Associates, *Achieving Excellence in Fund Raising: A Comprehensive Guide to Principles, Strategies, and Methods*. San Francisco: Jossey-Bass, 1991.

Sandeen, A. *The Chief Student Affairs Officer: Leader, Manager, Mediator, Educator*. San Francisco: Jossey-Bass, 1991.

Schuh, J. H., and Rickard, S. T. "Planning and Budgeting." In U. Delworth, G. R. Hanson, and Associates, *Student Services: A Handbook for the Profession*. (2nd ed.) San Francisco: Jossey-Bass, 1989.

Williamson, M. L., and Mamarchev, H. L. "A Systems Approach to Financial Management in Student Affairs." *NASPA Journal*, 1990, 27 (3), 199–205.

JAMES A. GOLD *is associate professor of educational foundations at the State University of New York College, Buffalo.*

DENNIS C. GOLDEN *is vice president for student affairs at the University of Louisville in Kentucky.*

THOMAS J. QUATROCHE *is professor of educational foundations and coordinator of the College Student Personnel Administration Program at the State University of New York College, Buffalo.*

This chapter presents specific, concrete recommendations for student affairs professionals looking to become involved in institutional advancement efforts. An annotated bibliography of key resources in this area is also provided.

Recommendations and Annotated Resources

Melvin C. Terrell, James A. Gold

Raising funds through institutional advancement initiatives is essential at most institutions of higher education to meet expenses. Along with private four-year institutions, state-supported four-year institutions are depending more on external funding. The trend toward privatization and reliance on external funds is widespread, since most states have not been able to support public higher education at prior levels.

Student affairs divisions, in particular, need additional funding to offer services and programs for students while sustaining budget shortfalls. This volume provides a number of recommendations for student affairs professionals interested in becoming involved in institutional advancement activities.

Recommendations

As part of the executive team, the chief student affairs officer (CSAO) should build strong personal and professional relationships with the chief institutional advancement officer (CIAO) and the president in order to be included in the institutional advancement initiative. It is important for the CSAO to coordinate efforts with the CIAO and to be sensitive to the reactions of the president and the CIAO when making a personal intervention with a donor. The president and the CIAO may be concerned that the effectiveness of their partnership will be compromised by the addition of other institutional professionals in the educational fundraising process. With more staff members meeting with donors, the president's relationships with the donors could be weakened.

To gain the president's support, the CSAO should present a realistic plan for achieving educational fundraising goals for student affairs within the context of the institution's mission. Include specific activities, staff time allotted to educational fundraising, a time line, and a cost-benefit analysis. Give assurance that staff will be able to fulfill their primary responsibilities to students.

Part of the plan should include new ways of structuring linkages with the institutional advancement office, such as assigning a staff person to attend institutional advancement office meetings (possibly with a shared salary arrangement). Include target areas in student affairs for institutional advancement initiatives, incentives to motivate staff, and a list of students or recent alumni who will assist with educational fundraising activities. Describe the plan to learn about the educational fundraising process, including the vocabulary and protocol associated with institutional advancement. Indicate how student affairs staff will be taught the requisite skills.

Annotated Resources

Brittingham, B. E., and Pezzullo, T. R. *The Campus Green: Fund Raising in Higher Education.* ASHE-ERIC Higher Education Reports, no. 1. Washington, D.C.: Association for the Study of Higher Education, 1990.

The authors provide an overview of the institutional advancement of educational fundraising in higher education and the changes that have occurred. The authors also report on research findings about educational fundraising and provide information on such topics as donor motivation, relationship between foundations and higher education, and the connection between intercollegiate athletics and educational fundraising. They also discuss future educational fundraising strategies for higher education administrators and trustees. The need for additional research in the field of higher educational fundraising is explicated.

Bryson, J. M. *Strategic Planning for Public and Nonprofit Organizations: A Guide to Strengthening and Sustaining Organizational Achievement.* San Francisco: Jossey-Bass, 1988.

The author's thesis is that strategic planning has defined ideas, procedures, and tools to help administrators and managers with the task of developing a strategic plan. While strategic planning has been used for a number of years, only recently has it been applied as a planning process for public and private nonprofit organizations. The book explains how to use strategic planning as a way of improving performance outcomes. The author also presents a successful strategic planning process for public and nonprofit organizations and describes how to overcome major problems in the strategic planning process. Examples of effective and ineffective strategic planning procedures are illustrated.

Dove, K. E. *Conducting a Successful Capital Campaign: A Comprehensive Fundraising Guide for Nonprofit Organizations.* San Francisco: Jossey-Bass, 1988.

This book describes the steps involved in establishing a successful capital campaign. The author provides information on such topics as selecting volunteers, constructing the campaign, identifying and rating campaign donors, and establishing day-to-day operations. At the end of the book, the author offers 103 examples of resources for a successful campaign. The book is useful for the experienced practitioner or for newcomers with limited capital campaign experience.

Keller, G. *Academic Strategy: The Management Revolution in American Higher Education.* Baltimore: Johns Hopkins University Press, 1983.

Based on a national study, this book discusses managerial transformation. The author defines the various management changes occurring in higher education. Presented in the first section of the book is a historical perspective of the changes and reforms that occurred in higher education. The author reviews participatory strategic planning that is being implemented at the more forward-thinking institutions, large and small, of higher education. The book provides a descriptive as well as a prescriptive view of strategic planning in higher education.

Rowland, A. W. (ed.). *Handbook of Institutional Advancement: A Modern Guide to Executive Management, Institutional Relations, Fund Raising, Alumni Administration, Government Relations, Publications, Periodicals, and Enrollment Management.* (2nd ed.) San Francisco: Jossey-Bass, 1986.

This publication provides extensive information for established professionals in as well as newcomers to the field of institutional advancement. The volume's subtitle lists the topics addressed. Institutional advancement programs are shown to help colleges and universities successfully perform their missions in a competitive environment as they gather available financial resources from a variety of sources. This publication can be extremely useful for institutions attempting to develop an effective, strategically planned capital campaign.

MELVIN C. TERRELL is vice president for student affairs and professor of counselor education at Northeastern Illinois University, Chicago.

JAMES A. GOLD is associate professor of educational foundations at the State University of New York College, Buffalo.

INDEX

ORDERING INFORMATION

NEW DIRECTIONS FOR STUDENT SERVICES is a series of paperback books that offers guidelines and programs for aiding students in their total development—emotional, social, and physical, as well as intellectual. Books in the series are published quarterly in Spring, Summer, Fall, and Winter, and are available for purchase by subscription and individually.

SUBSCRIPTIONS for 1993 cost $47.00 for individuals (a savings of 25 percent over single-copy prices) and $62.00 for institutions, agencies, and libraries. Please do not send institutional checks for personal subscriptions. Standing orders are accepted.

SINGLE COPIES cost $15.95 when payment accompanies order. (California, New Jersey, New York, and Washington, D.C., residents please include appropriate sales tax.) Billed orders will be charged postage and handling.

DISCOUNTS for quantity orders are available. Please write to the address below for information.

ALL ORDERS must include either the name of an individual or an official purchase order number. Please submit your order as follows:
   Subscriptions: specify series and year subscription is to begin
   Single copies: include individual title code (such as SS1)

MAIL ALL ORDERS TO:
   Jossey-Bass Publishers
   350 Sansome Street
   San Francisco, California 94104

FOR SINGLE-COPY SALES OUTSIDE OF THE UNITED STATES CONTACT:
   Maxwell Macmillan International Publishing Group
   866 Third Avenue
   New York, New York 10022

FOR SUBSCRIPTION SALES OUTSIDE OF THE UNITED STATES contact any international subscription agency or Jossey-Bass directly.

OTHER TITLES AVAILABLE IN THE
NEW DIRECTIONS FOR STUDENT SERVICES SERIES
Margaret J. Barr, Editor-in-Chief
M. Lee Upcraft, Associate Editor